Entrepreneurship Education and Student Empowerment

A scholarly work that explores the intersection of entrepreneurship education, innovation, and student empowerment within the European Union, this book investigates the transition from student to entrepreneur. It provides an in-depth analysis of the theoretical and empirical aspects of entrepreneurship education. With a field approach, including case studies and a quantitative review of university-level entrepreneurship courses across Europe, it offers a robust framework for fostering entrepreneurial skills and understanding how entrepreneurship education fosters innovation within the EU. It explores key factors driving student entrepreneurship, offering insights into the development of essential competencies such as soft skills, technical knowledge, and interpersonal abilities. Through practical applications, the book bridges the gap between education, research, and practice, providing practical recommendations for enhancing entrepreneurship education across Europe. Targeted towards academics, postgraduate students, and practitioners interested in entrepreneurship, edutech, and educational dynamics, it is particularly relevant to scholars in entrepreneurship education and innovation, offering valuable insights into how to empower students and foster entrepreneurial ecosystems in the EU.

Chiara Bartoli is Research Fellow at the Research Center in Strategic Change "Franco Fontana" at LUISS Guido Carli University. She is Adjunct Professor of Corporate Strategy and Megatrends at LUISS Guido Carli University. Her research interests include digital entrepreneurship, strategic agility, new technologies, and business model innovation with a focus on Web 3.0, metaverse, artificial intelligence, and blockchain.

Federica Brunetta is Associate Professor of Management. She teaches general management, strategy, economics of strategy, and business transformation at Luiss Business School and at the Department of Business and Management at Luiss Guido Carli University. She is Head of Executive Masters of Luiss Business School and Vice Director of the Research Centre in Strategic Change "Franco Fontana" of Luiss University. Her research interests are focused on the study of strategies in highly regulated environments, digitalization and business transformation, and network analysis. Her works are published, among others, in *Organization Studies*, *Journal of Business Research*, *IEEE Transactions on Engineering Management*, *Technological Forecasting, and Social Change*.

Routledge Focus on Business and Management

The fields of business and management have grown exponentially as areas of research and education. This growth presents challenges for readers trying to keep up with the latest important insights. *Routledge Focus on Business and Management* presents small books on big topics and how they intersect with the world of business research.

Individually, each title in the series provides coverage of a key academic topic, whilst collectively, the series forms a comprehensive collection across the business disciplines.

Digital Entrepreneurship and Disruptive Innovation
Intersections of Regional Development, Innovation Systems, and Sustainability
Jordi Diaz, Daphne Halkias and Tatiana Harkiolakis

Organisational Flexibility in an Age of Chaos
Mismanagement, Disorganisation and Strategy
Andrés Hatum

Sustainable Organizational Change
The Social Change Model for Systems
Joshua D. Burton and Barbara Carter

Entrepreneurship Education and Student Empowerment
Innovation in the EU
Chiara Bartoli and Federica Brunetta

For more information about this series, please visit: www.routledge.com/Routledge-Focus-on-Business-and-Management/book-series/FBM

Entrepreneurship Education and Student Empowerment

Innovation in the EU

Chiara Bartoli and Federica Brunetta

Routledge
Taylor & Francis Group
NEW YORK AND LONDON

First published 2026
by Routledge
605 Third Avenue, New York, NY 10158

and by Routledge
4 Park Square, Milton Park, Abingdon, Oxon, OX14 4RN

Routledge is an imprint of the Taylor & Francis Group, an informa business

ISBN: 978-1-032-98740-8 (hbk)
ISBN: 978-1-003-86420-2 (pbk)
ISBN: 978-1-003-60764-9 (ebk)

DOI: 10.4324/9781003607649

The Open Access version of Chapters 4 and 5 was funded by Divisione Luiss Business School.

For Product Safety Concerns and Information please contact our EU representative: GPSR@taylorandfrancis.com
Taylor & Francis Verlag GmbH,
Kaufingerstraße 24,
80331 München, Germany.

Contents

Figures

Tables

Contributors

Chapter 3. Framing a European model of entrepreneurship education
- Paola Belingheri, Luiss Guido Carli University
- Christian Lechner, Luiss Guido Carli University

Chapter 4. Collaborative strategies for student entrepreneurship: from mentoring to venture building
- Abel Fernandez, EBAN
- Jacopo Piccagli, EBAN
- Paola Belingheri, Luiss Guido Carli University
- Christian Lechner, Luiss Guido Carli University
- Katrin Singer-Coudoux, Fraunhofer IPK
- Henry Nicolai Buxmann, Fraunhofer IPK

Chapter 5. Entrepreneurship education to foster innovation: the role of hackathons
- Katerina Zargani – Corallia, Athens, Greece
- Nektaria Berikou – Corallia, Athens, Greece
- Nikos Vogiatzis – Corallia, Athens, Greece
- Jorge-A. Sanchez-P. – Corallia, Athens, Greece
- Paola Belingheri, Luiss Guido Carli University
- Christian Lechner, Luiss Guido Carli University

Chapter 6. New technological trends in entrepreneurship education
- Lorenza Gerardi – Research Fellow of the Research Center for Strategic Change "Franco Fontana".

Acknowledgments

This work is the result of studies that were conducted as part of the project ENTREPRENEDU, funded by the European Union under the Grant Agreement 101100507.

We thank all ENTREPRENEDU Partners.

We would also like to thank Prof. Christian Lechner, Full Professor of Entrepreneurship and Director of the Department of Business and Management at Luiss Guido Carli, for his valuable guidance and insights during writing of the book.

Special thanks also go to the Research Centre in Strategic Change "Franco Fontana" of Luiss Guido Carli University and to the Director, Prof. Enzo Peruffo and the President Prof. Paolo Boccardelli.

Introduction

Student entrepreneurs have emerged as one important trend that has attracted the attention of both the business and academic worlds, thanks to famous cases of successful companies created in university environments, such as Facebook, founded by Mark Zuckerberg and some of his classmates. Other famous student founders include Larry Page and Sergey Brin, who created Google during their PhD studies at Stanford, and Jerry Yang, who launched Yahoo! while still in college.

Indeed, young entrepreneurs are redefining the rules of the game of innovation. Their energy, creativity, and ability to innovate give rise to successful start-ups, fuel innovation ecosystems, accelerate the digital transformation, and strengthen economic resilience. For these reasons, the topic of youth entrepreneurial activity and the phenomenon of student entrepreneurship have gained increasing attention from both the academic and business worlds.

In Europe, student entrepreneurship is expanding rapidly. More and more young students are launching businesses with a digital-first approach, combining advanced technological skills with a strong focus on social impact. In this context, the EU has shown growing interest in youth entrepreneurship as a strategic tool to strengthen economic and social resilience, promote sustainability, and stimulate competitiveness and innovation.

While there is a willingness to create new ventures among young Europeans, there are also inhibiting factors that can limit the effectiveness of entrepreneurial learning pathways. Understanding the factors and mechanisms that determine the acceleration of the transition from idea to creation of new entrepreneurial ventures among young learners is crucial for strengthening the processes of innovation and

DOI: 10.4324/9781003607649-1

development of EU competitiveness. In light of this, this volume aims to contribute to the knowledge on youth empowerment by exploring ways to develop entrepreneurial skills and support the transition to self-employment. The aim of this volume is to provide the reader with an understanding of the phenomenon of student entrepreneurship in Europe and beyond, through an analysis of its dimensions and implications, with a focus on the role of university and entrepreneurship education.

In particular, the work provides an in-depth analysis of student entrepreneurship and entrepreneurship education and research in Europe. It offers a systematic review of the literature to understand the factors that facilitate and hinder student entrepreneurship. Through a benchmarking analysis of the main entrepreneurial courses provided by European universities, it builds a comprehensive framework for successful entrepreneurial learning, which is pivotal for fostering entrepreneurial ideas in the business ecosystem. By doing so, it emphasizes the crucial link between research and practices in the entrepreneurial sphere.

The book also reports on the innovative initiatives of entrepreneurship education of the European project ENTREPRENEDU, thus providing practical tools and a useful guide for universities wishing to implement innovative methodologies for entrepreneurship education.

Furthermore, the work provides a comprehensive overview of emerging trends in entrepreneurship education that are closely associated with the development of digital technologies, paying particular attention to AI, blockchain, and the metaverse.

It offers academic and education manager and entrepreneurs with the opportunity to dive into the complexities of student entrepreneurship and gain critical insights into its multifaceted nature. This undertaking encompasses the examination of the emerging technological landscape, which is poised to significantly impact the field. The book seeks to empower readers by equipping them with a thorough comprehension of the subject matter, thereby fostering their ability to engage meaningfully with the evolving phenomenon of student entrepreneurship.

1 Student entrepreneurship

A European and global perspective

1.1 Student entrepreneurship: an overview

Student entrepreneurs are a specific type of businessperson with a unique approach to acquiring and using resources as compared to entrepreneurs who start businesses outside of the university setting (Politis et al., 2012). By acting as entrepreneurs, university students foster the creation of networks that support the emergence of new small and medium-sized enterprises. They also accelerate knowledge transfer processes that favor not only active exchanges between universities and businesses but also the creation of innovative new ecosystems (Ayala-Gaytán et al., 2024) while also supporting regional development (Cho et al., 2024; Passavanti et al., 2023).

In the process of transforming young students into entrepreneurs, universities play an essential role, not limited to the creation of university spin-offs or to transferring knowledge to students through lectures. In fact, there are examples especially from the United States showing how universities can create an environment where knowledge and practical experience intersect, cultivating an entrepreneurial mindset among students and giving them the skills to create new ventures (Secundo et al., 2020).

1.1.1 Data on universities and student founders

Data from the Visual Capitalist report[1] show that the top universities in terms of the number of founders are predominantly located in the United States and Great Britain. During the 2022/2023 academic year, Stanford University, MIT, and the University of California, Berkeley, emerged as the leading institutions in terms of start-up creation by

DOI: 10.4324/9781003607649-2

students. Notably, UC Berkeley stands out in terms of the number of entrepreneurs among undergraduates (1,811), followed by Stanford (1,547) and Harvard. Similarly, Stanford emerged as the leading university in terms of founders among graduate students (4,214), followed by Harvard (3,716) and MIT (2,834). Berkeley's superiority in fostering start-up creation, which is backed up by the statistics, can be attributed to its strategic location near Silicon Valley. This proximity, in turn, facilitates access to a pervasive entrepreneurial culture, thereby underscoring the significance of external factors in the successful establishment of companies by young founders at academic institutions (Nickie, 2024; Figure 1.1).

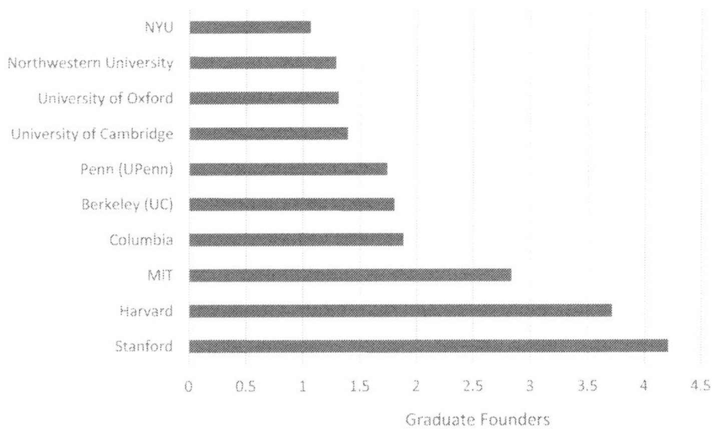

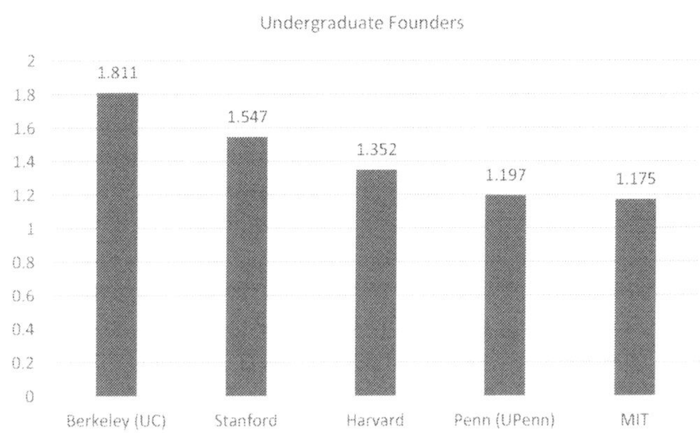

Figure 1.1 Top universities by start-up founders, including undergraduates and graduate students.

Source: adapted from Visual Capitalist.

The significant concentration of new entrepreneurial ventures created at major universities in the United States is also due to a well-established entrepreneurial culture and to the great emphasis on entrepreneurship courses as part of university curricula. Actually, many business and technology schools in the United States have created "concentrations" or "majors" in entrepreneurship, establishing themselves as a valuable niche for new venture creation (Wilson, 2008). In addition, there are entire university departments dedicated to entrepreneurship, along with university facilities that support students in coming up with and experimenting with new ideas. Furthermore, a sort of osmosis process is being created between student entrepreneurs and their universities. In fact, through the founding of start-ups, graduates, and students actively contribute to the innovation process and participate in the creation and transfer of new knowledge from the university to the market. This strengthens universities' knowledge transfer processes and reinforces their reputation as entrepreneurial universities (Boh et al., 2016).

1.1.2 Student entrepreneurship: global data

Global statistics confirm the university students' attitude toward the creation of new ventures. Specifically, the GUESS Global Report[2] shows that, in 2023, 15.7% of students at the global level intended to become entrepreneurs immediately after their studies ("direct intentional entrepreneurs"), while, 5 years after the completion of studies, this percentage increased to 30% of graduates who planned to be entrepreneurs (Figure 1.2) with a sharp decline in the propensity to become employees from 65% to 53%.[3]

When it comes to entrepreneurial activities during their studies, approximately 10% of the students surveyed reported being active entrepreneurs, while 25.7% of the total sample ($N = 58,314$) indicated that they were "currently engaged" in attempting to establish their own business in collaboration with other cofounders. These students are therefore designated as "nascent entrepreneurs." Furthermore, nearly one-third of nascent entrepreneurs expressed a desire to complete this founding activity during their university studies. Furthermore, what emerges is that almost the majority of students (47.1%) intended to pursue their entrepreneurial endeavors after completing their studies (Sieger et al., 2024).

One important finding from the Guess Database is that young individuals frequently opt to first work as hired employees prior to embarking upon an entrepreneurial career. This transition typically occurs in a gradual manner. Nevertheless, a comparison of the shares of nascent entrepreneurs in the surveyed countries indicates that

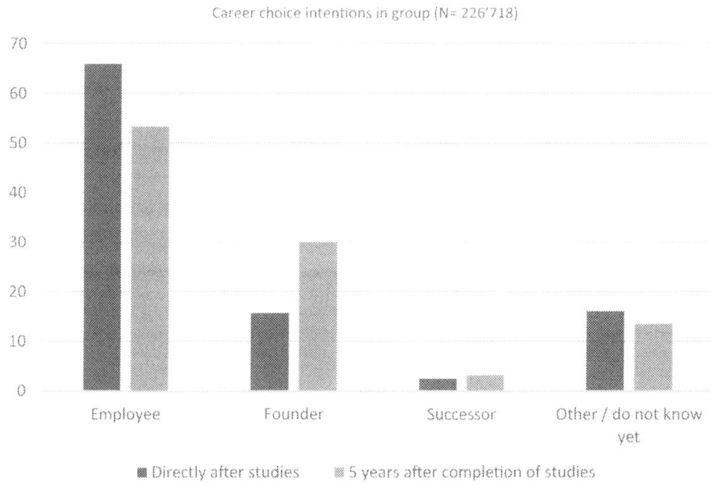

Figure 1.2 Students' entrepreneurial career choice intentions.
Source: GUESSS 2023 Global Report.

developing countries are often at the top of the list, accounting for the highest rates of intentions to become founders right after one's studies. Developed countries, on the other hand, rank lowest. Furthermore, the geographical distribution of new ventures also offers insights into the role of location in entrepreneurial endeavors. Data show a preference among start-up founders for the city where they are currently studying, with 54.3% of new ventures being established in the same city where students reside.[4]

The university environment and the specific field of study appear to play a pivotal role in shaping student entrepreneurship. Notably, those who have pursued studies in "*Business and Management*" show a higher propensity for becoming entrepreneurs compared to those pursuing other areas of study. This can be seen in Figure 1.3. This aspect suggests that the content and structure of university courses may also influence the intention to launch a start-up.

1.1.3 Student entrepreneurs in the European context

From a European perspective, official statistics[5] show that young Europeans are familiar with the concept of entrepreneurship (12% being "*very much*" familiar and 35% "*quite a bit*" familiar). This goes

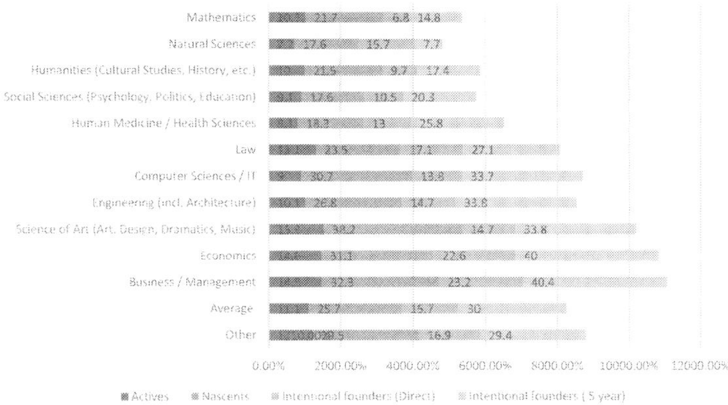

Figure 1.3 Entrepreneurial intentions and activities depending on field of study (%).

Source: GUESSS 2023 Global Report.

hand in hand with the attitude towards being an entrepreneur. In fact, 39% of young Europeans would prefer self-employment and believe that being an entrepreneur is a hallmark of their generation, with data showing that young Europeans believe that their peers are interested in starting their own businesses (with 48% "quite interested" and 20% "very interested"). The decision to become an entrepreneur mainly has to do with the perception of the greater independence in one's work that entrepreneurship offers (49%), combined with the freedom to choose where and how to work. Furthermore, young Europeans believe that entrepreneurs have the following characteristics: courage (34%), ambition (32%), and the ability to create jobs (30%).

Statistics reveal a unique data point in the approach young Europeans take to entrepreneurship: there is a significant gap between intention and actual behavior. In fact, while many young people would consider starting their own business, this attitude rarely translates into the creation of a new business, as few of the young people surveyed are self-employed. Only 9% have already started a business, and 14% are taking the necessary steps to start a business. These data reflect OECD figures about so-called "missing" entrepreneurs who account for 44% of the total number of active entrepreneurs in the EU and 34% in OECD countries (Table 1.1).[6]

Table 1.1 Attitude of young Europeans toward entrepreneurship

Percentage	*Description*
39	Would prefer being self-employed
46	Would consider starting up a new business
14	Are taking steps to start a business
9	Are self-employed

Source: Social Entrepreneurship and Youth Report, Oct 2022.

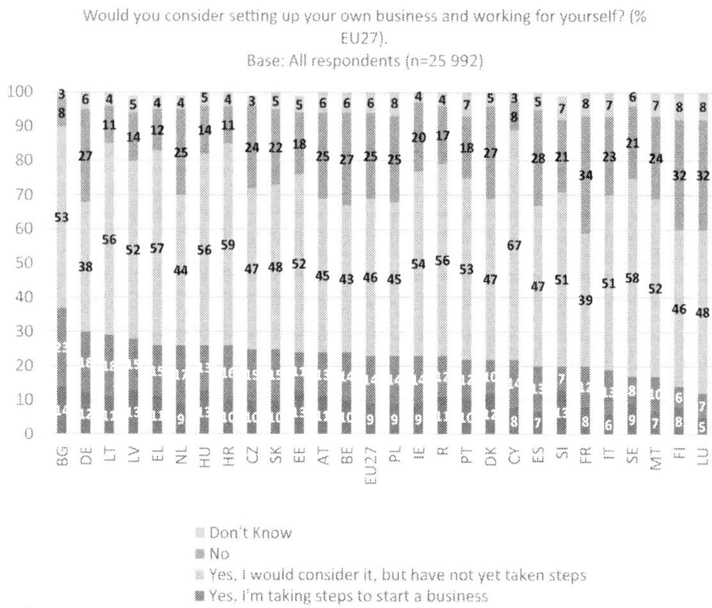

Figure 1.4 Attitude of young Europeans toward Entrepreneurship. Country comparison.

Source: Social Entrepreneurship and Youth Report, Oct 2022.

However, disparities exist in some demographic groups, particularly among women and young people, as well as among different European countries. In fact, European statistics show that the youth self-employment rate is highest in countries like Bulgaria (14%), Hungary (13%), Latvia (13%), and Slovenia (13%), while it is very low in other countries, such as Spain (7%), Italy (6%), and Luxemburg (5%).[7]

Moreover, young Europeans who expressed a desire to start their own businesses also identified a specific industry they would focus on, including IT, the Internet, e-commerce, or social media (13%), followed by arts, design, culture (10%), commerce, trade and retail (9%), hospitality, entertainment, and tourism (9%).

1.2 Individual factors affecting student entrepreneurship

1.2.1 The role of motivation

Data confirm the importance of student entrepreneurship as a growing phenomenon, with young people showing a greater propensity for starting businesses than other generations (Sieger et al., 2024). Therefore, student entrepreneurs can serve to drive entrepreneurship globally and help bridge the existing innovation gap (Boh et al., 2016). However, students are not always successful in running their businesses; in fact, recent OECD-EU data from the Missing Entrepreneurs project shows that many young people are being held back from realizing their full entrepreneurial potential (OECD/European Commission, 2023). This has recently led the academy to focus on understanding what internal and external factors underpin the success of youth-founded entrepreneurial ventures.

The academic literature agrees that entrepreneurial success lies not only in motivations, as there is a multiplicity of determinants that must be taken into account and that have an impact on the willingness of students to become entrepreneurs. Other factors come into play at individual (e.g., skills and competencies, and personality traits), interpersonal (e.g., networking, family, and social norms), and societal (e.g., government policies, regulations, the educational context, and the economic scenario) levels (Maheshwari et al., 2022).

Therefore, these aspects could influence course curricula and need to be taken into account to ensure the effectiveness of training aimed at empowering student entrepreneurs (António Porfírio et al., 2023), as venture building by young university students could be the result of the interplay between personal mindset and attitude with the availability of external resources (Linder et al., 2019).[8]

Entrepreneurial motivation is recognized as the driving force that prompts an individual to translate the intention to start a business venture into concrete actions. In their work, Le and Tran (2021) suggested that entrepreneurial motivation could be categorized into two main types: extrinsic motivation and intrinsic motivation. Extrinsic motivation is fueled by external factors, such as family, friends, and important individuals who offer support. While these external elements can influence the decision to embark upon an entrepreneurial journey, they are often linked to tangible rewards or societal pressures. Intrinsic motivation stems from a deep inner drive and is fueled by passion, personal challenge, and individual fulfillment. Students exhibit strong intrinsic motivation when they intend to start a business, demonstrating a profound interest, a sense of excitement, and determination in pursuing their entrepreneurial goals. Youth entrepreneurial motivation also results from the need to fulfill dreams, make a difference, and create something significant of one's own (Le and Tran, 2021).

Researchers have emphasized that motivations may also depend on the country of origin of students. For example, the study by Pruett et al. (2009) compared the motivations of students in universities in the United States, Spain, and China. They showed that Chinese students put more emphasis on social status and money motivations than on the entrepreneurial independence aspect that is prevalent among American and European students. For the Europeans, on the other hand, "dissatisfaction with one's job" and "difficulty in finding the right job" are seen as the main motivations for starting a new business.

1.2.2 The role of personal characteristics

Management literature recognizes the relevance of individual traits and characteristics as factors influencing the entrepreneurial tendencies of students (Bolton and Lane, 2012). To this point, Pruett et al. (2009) further demonstrates that the predisposition for entrepreneurship is linked to one's level of independence and the opportunity for creative work.

Furthermore, in studying the behavior of university students, Junça-Silva et al. (2024) showed that creativity is only one aspect that acts alongside other individual characteristics, such as personal initiative and risk-taking. These three personal characteristics are synergistic activators of the ability of young students to discover and recognize new opportunities for novel ventures.

Literature points out that individuals showing higher risk tolerance feel more capable and confident in entrepreneurial pursuits and show greater entrepreneurial intentions (Maheshwari et al., 2022). To this point, Al-Qadasi et al. (2024) add self-efficacy as a key facilitator of student entrepreneurial initiatives and a significant driver of entrepreneurial intention. Scholars have also remarked on the pivotal role played by the personal characteristic of "innovativeness," which is seen as the propensity to experiment with new ideas and new industries (Harris and Gibson, 2008). Along with the attitude toward entrepreneurship, this forms what Galvão et al. (2020) called "Individual Entrepreneurial Orientation (IEO)." This is a personal characteristic that fosters the ability to discover new opportunities. Therefore, IEO includes the methods, practices, and decision-making styles that individual use when acting in an entrepreneurial way. According to the author, students with high IEO have the ability to identify and explore new opportunities in the marketplace (Galvão et al., 2020). The authors also demonstrate how entrepreneurial orientation can be considered a personal expression of a soft skill, one that can be developed in higher education through appropriate entrepreneurship education (Galvão et al., 2020).

However, personal characteristics can also hinder student entrepreneurial orientation and innovation. The work carried out by Baldo et al. (2023) recognizes that "fear of failure" and "resistance to change" can act as cognitive barriers to student entrepreneurship. These barriers are more pronounced among people who have experienced economic crises or shocks, and among rural students who view risk-taking as an internal barrier to entrepreneurial orientation. These factors might increase the lack of confidence that discourages young students from taking further steps for venture creation. These constraints may be perceived at a higher level by those students who lack specific competencies to start a business internally.

Knowledge and competencies related to business start-ups can influence the aptitude to create a start-up. Hence, those students who have fewer skills that are required for business start-ups may run into more obstacles in starting a new venture than those who have taken entrepreneurship courses (Santos et al., 2019). This confirms the results of statistics on the areas of study of young entrepreneurs, who come prevalently from the faculties of business and economics (Sieger et al., 2024).

An emerging area of student entrepreneurship focuses on the impact of perceived well-being when it comes to students starting businesses. Hahn's (2020) study added that psychological capital and self-care are two personal resources fundamental to personal well-being, serving as key drivers of entrepreneurial success. These characteristics can be considered valuable assets in preparing future entrepreneurs to effectively manage risk and uncertainties. These factors are inherent in the process of establishing a novel enterprise. The author suggests that these competencies should be taught to students as soft skills (Hahn, 2020).

1.2.3 The role of culture and gender

The propensity to become an entrepreneur may also vary by gender and culture. Males and females have different approaches to entrepreneurship (Purwana et al., 2017). The study by Harris and Gibson (2008)—which examined the personality traits of a sample of 216 male students enrolled in American colleges—found that while male students scored higher on both personal control and innovation, women were less inclined to start innovative ventures and more likely to start businesses in sectors with a lower risk of failure, such as retail. This suggests that courses need to be designed to give female students a higher tolerance for risk in order to steer their choices towards the creation of innovative ventures.

Cultural values are another factor that influences the propensity to become an entrepreneur. These refer to a set of shared values that shape individual behavior within society (Inglehart, 1997). Hence, a national culture that fosters entrepreneurship can enhance the perceived legitimacy of the entrepreneur, thereby facilitating the development of entrepreneurial characteristics and psychological traits. (Ayob, 2023). For instance, Cruz (2022) demonstrated that, while the values of embeddedness and harmony positively influence entrepreneurial intention, the values of egalitarianism, affective autonomy, and intellectual autonomy have a negative correlation with entrepreneurial intention.

1.3 Relational conditions influencing entrepreneurial intentions

Studies also observed the relational aspects that pertain to the student's context and may determine the construction of a certain individual approach to entrepreneurship (Bergmann et al., 2016; Maheshwari et al., 2022).

1.3.1 Social factors

Social factors that can influence entrepreneurial intention include social norms, which could guide how the entrepreneur's activity is recognized within the student network (Giannetti and Simonov, 2004).

Specifically, in their study, Dohse and Walter (2012) emphasized the importance of the social capital that individuals can gather. This can be formed through existing personal ties, through the network of friends, family members, or other acquaintances.

1.3.1.1 Influence of family

Family background and previous entrepreneurial activity at the family level may play a role in fostering student entrepreneurship. Fairlie and Robb (2007) found that children of entrepreneurs are more likely to become entrepreneurs themselves. Previous experience in the family business is recognized as having a positive impact on individuals' perceptions of the feasibility and desirability of starting a new business (Peterman and Kennedy, 2003). Direct exposure to past entrepreneurial activity is considered a key factor in enhancing entrepreneurial intention. Therefore, young people who grow up in families of entrepreneurs show higher levels of innovativeness and personal achievement (Harris and Gibson, 2008). Conversely, Pruett et al. (2009) saw family as being a social barrier. This social barrier can be linked to the cultural predisposition to entrepreneurship, where personal failure not only affects the individual but also impacts the group. This makes the fear of failure more significant in countries where a collectivist culture prevails than in countries where a more individualistic culture is prevalent.

1.3.1.2 The role of the network

One's network is seen as an emergent social factor in the context of student entrepreneurship (Rasmussen et al., 2015). This is considered particularly relevant in the early stages of venture creation. Specifically, the network formed in the university environment plays a crucial role in enhancing knowledge resources and skill acquisition, which are vital for recognizing and pursuing business opportunities. Recent studies have recognized how such a network evolves over time. At the same time, universities represent a place for the creation and development of new networks that support the future development of ideas even outside the university context (Rasmussen et al., 2015).

1.3.2 Role models and mentoring

Scholars place importance on role models that can guide the creation of a new venture, as demonstrated by the work of Jin et al. (2023). The authors analyzed the behavior of over 500 university students in China, showing that role models exert a positive influence on the propensity to becoming entrepreneurs. This happens because they inspire and motivate students to get involved in entrepreneurial activities and create a style that can be imitated by future entrepreneurs (Gibson, 2004). When deciding to create a start-up, students need to look at the success of their peers (Jin et al., 2023).

Mentoring is another tool considered to be a driver for student entrepreneurship. This exchange helps support the transfer of knowledge when it comes to doing business, improving the ability of students to recognize and leverage market opportunities (Gimmon, 2014; Ozgen and Baron, 2007).

The effectiveness of mentoring is particularly pronounced when mentors come from the business world, as they enhance students' sense of empowerment by fostering psychological security and boosting self-confidence. However, the impact of mentoring can vary based on students' cultural backgrounds and personality traits (St-Jean et al., 2017).

1.4 Situational factors influencing entrepreneurial intentions

Contextual factors are external circumstances and environmental aspects that can influence the intentions of students when it comes to starting a new entrepreneurial venture.

External factors that can influence student entrepreneurship may be related to access to financial resources and regulatory or administrative barriers in a specific regional context. An external context characterized by the presence of institutional support and an environment that financially supports start-ups can increase the confidence of new entrepreneurs and reduce the perceived risk of failure among students (Jyoti et al., 2011). Scholars further suggest that these aspects are more likely to impact students from rural areas, where there is a greater perception of barriers to entrepreneurship, as well as students living in areas where there is no access to local business communities. These students are therefore less likely to gain experience, confidence, and innovative skills (Baldo et al., 2023).

What's more, the work of Dohse and Walter (2012) shows that student entrepreneurship is influenced by the business environment. The authors focus on two major factors: the concentration of start-ups and investment in research and development (R&D). Specifically, when a region has a high density of start-ups and significant investment in R&D, the processes of generating new knowledge improve, creating a more conducive environment for aspiring entrepreneurs. Indeed, an environment characterized by innovation dynamism generates knowledge spillovers, where the benefits of innovation spread to other players in the ecosystem and increases the ability of new entrepreneurs to leverage existing research and development to create successful businesses.

1.5 Conclusions

Student entrepreneurship is a multidimensional phenomenon that represents an important lever for economic development since it creates the conditions for strengthening the circulation of knowledge. Student entrepreneurship is influenced by several factors that enable the transformation of a student into an entrepreneur, among which assume relevance the social and personality factors, as well as the context and relationship with the business environment.

In the process of transforming students into entrepreneurs, universities play a fundamental role as a bridge between private initiative and the realization of ideas. In fact, it is in universities, through entrepreneurship training, that theoretical learning is integrated with real-world applications and where students can create solid networks with the business world. Therefore, especially at the European level, universities act as innovation hubs to promote entrepreneurial success by transforming the propensity to become entrepreneurs into action.

Notes

1 Visual Capitalist report, "Which Universities Produce the Most Start-up Founders", September 2024. Available at: www.visualcapitalist.com/which-universities-produce-the-most-startup-founders/
2 The Guess Database report documents the results of an annual survey involving more than 226,000 students in 57 countries.
3 GUESS Global Report, 2023. Available at: www.guesssurvey.org/resources/PDF_InterReports/GUESSS_2023_Global_Report.pdf
4 *GUESS Global Report, 2023. Available at:* www.guesssurvey.org/resources/PDF_InterReports/GUESSS_2023_GlobalReport.pdf
5 Flash Eurobarometer 513 Social Entrepreneurship and Youth—October 2022. Published in March 2023.
6 The Missing Entrepreneurs 2023. Policies for Inclusive Entrepreneurship and Self-Employment, November 2023. Available at: www.oecd.org/en/publications/the-missing-entrepreneurs-2023_230efc78-en.html
7 Flash Eurobarometer 513 Social Entrepreneurship and Youth—October 2022.
8 GEM (Global Entrepreneurship Monitor) (2023). Global Entrepreneurship Monitor 2022/2023 Global Report: Adapting to a "New Normal". London: GEM. Avalaible at: www.gemconsortium.org/

References

Al-Qadasi, N., Zhang, G., Al-Jubari, I., Al-Awlaqi, M.A. and Aamer, A.M. (2024). "Entrepreneurship education and entrepreneurial behaviour: Do self-efficacy and attitude matter?", *International Journal of Management Education*, Vol. 22, No. 1, 100945.

António Porfírio, J., Augusto Felício, J., Carrilho, T. and Jardim, J. (2023). "Promoting entrepreneurial intentions from adolescence: The influence of entrepreneurial culture and education", *Journal of Business Research*, Vol. 156, 113521.

Ayala-Gaytán, E., Villasana, M. and Naranjo-Priego, E.E. (2024). "University entrepreneurial ecosystems and graduate entrepreneurship", *Journal of Entrepreneurship*, Vol. 33, No. 1, pp. 88–117.

Ayob, A.H. (2023). "Institutions and student entrepreneurship: The effects of economic conditions, culture and education", *Educational Studies*, Vol. 00, No. 00, pp. 1–19.

Baldo, C.M., Chen McCain, S.-L. and Jouflas, G. (2023). "An investigation on factors influencing University students' entrepreneurship orientations", *Entrepreneurship Education and Pedagogy*, Vol. 7, No. 3, pp. 264–288.

", *Small Business Economics*, Vol. 47, pp.57–79 https://doi.org/10.1007/s11187-016-9700-6

Boh, W.F., De-Haan, U. and Strom, R. (2016). "University technology transfer through entrepreneurship: Faculty and students in spinoffs", *Journal of Technology Transfer*, Vol. 41, No. 4, pp. 661–669.

Bolton, D. L., & Lane, M. D. (2012). Individual entrepreneurial orientation: Development of a measurement instrument. *Education & Training*, Vol. 54(2-3), pp. 219–233. https://doi.org/10.1108/00400911211210314

Cho, D.S., Owalla, B. and Ge, B. (2024). "Entrepreneurs in residence at the nexus of regional economy and university entrepreneurial ecosystems", *Regional Studies, Regional Science*, Vol. 11, No. 1, pp. 441–452.

Cruz, P.D.A. (2022). "La influencia de los valores culturales en la intención emprededora en estudiantes de educación superior", *RIDE Revista Iberoamericana Para La Investigación y El Desarrollo Educativo*, Vol. 13, No. 25 SE-Artículos Científicos. https://doi.org/10.23913/ride.v13i25.1319.

Dohse, D. and Walter, S.G. (2012). "Knowledge context and entrepreneurial intentions among students", *Small Business Economics*, Vol. 39, No. 4, pp. 877–895.

Fairlie, R.W. and Robb, A. (2007). "Families, human capital, and small business: evidence from the characteristics of business owners survey", *ILR Review*, Vol. 60, No. 2, pp. 225–245.

Galvão, A., Marques, C. and Ferreira, J.J. (2020). "The role of entrepreneurship education and training programmes in advancing entrepreneurial skills and new ventures", *European Journal of Training and Development*, Vol. 44, No. 6/7, pp. 595–614.

Giannetti, M. and Simonov, A. (2004). "On the determinants of entrepreneurial activity: Social norms, economic environment, and individual characteristics", *Swedish Economic Policy Review*, Vol. 11, pp. 269–313.

Gibson, D.E. (2004). "Role models in career development: New directions for theory and research", *Journal of Vocational Behavior*, Vol. 65, No. 1, pp. 134–156.

Gimmon, E. (2014). "Mentoring as a practical training in higher education of entrepreneurship", *Education + Training*, Vol. 56, pp. 814–825.

Hahn, D. (2020). "The psychological well-being of student entrepreneurs: A social identity perspective", *International Entrepreneurship and Management Journal*, Vol. 16 No. 2, pp. 467–499.

Harris, M.L. and Gibson, S.G. (2008). "Examining the entrepreneurial attitudes of US business students", *Education + Training*, Vol. 50, No. 7, pp. 568–581.

Inglehart, R. (1997). *Modernization and Postmodernization.* Princeton University Press. https://doi.org/10.2307/j.ctv10vm2ns

Jin, D., Liu, X., Zhang, F. and Wen, Z. (2023). "Entrepreneurial role models and college students' entrepreneurial calling: A moderated mediation model", *Frontiers in Psychology*, Vol. 14, No. February, pp. 1–17.

Jyoti, J., Sharma, J., & Kumari, A. (2011). Factors affecting orientation and satisfaction of women entrepreneurs in rural India. *Annals of Innovation & Entrepreneurship,* Vol. 2(1). https://doi.org/10.3402/aie.v2i1.7371

Junça-Silva, A., Duarte, H. and Santos, S.C. (2024). "Personal initiative, risk-taking, creativity and opportunity discovery among students", *Journal of Enterprising Communities: People and Places in the Global Economy*, Vol. 18, No. 1, pp. 49–71.

Le, T.T.K. and Tran, B.T. (2021). "Entrepreneurial Motivations and Intentions among Students: A Case Study at a Vocational Institution". In *ICETT 2021: 2021 7th International Conference on Education and Training Technologies*. Acau, China.

Linder, C., Lechner, C. and Pelzel, F. (2019). "Many roads lead to Rome: How human, social, and financial capital are related to new venture survival", *Entrepreneurship Theory and Practice*, Vol. 44, 104225871986755.

Maheshwari, G., Kha, K.L. and Arokiasamy, A.R.A. (2022). "Factors affecting students' entrepreneurial intentions: A systematic review (2005–2022) for future directions in theory and practice", *Management Review Quarterly*, Vol. 73, pp. 1903–1970. https://doi.org/10.1007/s11301-022-00289-2

Nickie, L. (2024). "Top universities that produce the most startup founders", *Tech Startups*. Available at: https://techstartups.com/2024/09/27/top-universities-that-produce-the-most-startup-founders/

OECD/European Commission. (2023). *The Missing Entrepreneurs 2023: Policies for Inclusive Entrepreneurship and Self-Employment.* OECD Publishing, Paris, https://doi.org/10.1787/230efc78-en

Ozgen, E. and Baron, R.A. (2007). "Social sources of information in opportunity recognition: effects of mentors, industry networks, and professional forums", *Journal of Business Venturing*, Vol. 22, No. 2, pp. 174–192.

Passavanti, C., Ponsiglione, C., Primario, S. and Rippa, P. (2023). "The evolution of student entrepreneurship: state of the art and emerging research direction", *The International Journal of Management Education*, Vol. 21, No. 2, 100820.

Peterman, N.E. and Kennedy, J. (2003). "Enterprise education: influencing students' perceptions of entrepreneurship", *Entrepreneurship Theory and Practice*, Vol. 28 No. 2, pp. 129–144.

Politis, D., Winborg, J. and Dahlstrand, Å.L. (2012). "Exploring the resource logic of student entrepreneurs", *International Small Business Journal*, Vol. 30, No. 6, pp. 659–683.

Pruett, M., Shinnar, R., Toney, B., Llopis, F. and Fox, J. (2009). "Explaining entrepreneurial intentions of university students: a cross-cultural study", *International Journal of Entrepreneurial Behavior & Research*, Vol. 15, No. 6, pp. 571–594.

Purwana, D., Suhud, U. and Rahayu, S. (2017). "Entrepreneurial Intention of secondary and tertiary students: are they different?", *International Journal of Economic Research*, Vol. 14 (18), pp. 69–81

Rasmussen, E., Mosey, S. and Wright, M. (2015). "The transformation of network ties to develop entrepreneurial competencies for university spin-offs", *Entrepreneurship & Regional Development*, Vol. 27, No. 7–8, pp. 430–457.

Santos, S.C., Neumeyer, X. and Morris, M.H. (2019), Entrepreneurship Education in a Poverty Context: An Empowerment Perspective. *J Small Bus Manag*, Vol. 57: 6-32. https://doi.org/10.1111/jsbm.12485

Secundo, G., Mele, G., Sansone, G. and Paolucci, E. (2020). "Entrepreneurship education centres in universities: evidence and insights from Italian 'Contamination Lab' cases", *International Journal of Entrepreneurial Behavior & Research*, Vol. 26, No. 6, pp. 1311–1333.

Sieger, P., Raemy, L., Zellweger, T., Fueglistaller, U. and Hatak, I. (2024). *Entrepreneurship 2023: Insights from 57 Countries. 2023 GUESSS Global Report. s. St.Gallen/Bern: KMU-HSG/IMU-U.*

St-Jean, É., Tremblay, M., Janssen, F., Baronet, J., Loué, C. and Nafa, A. (2017). "May business mentors act as opportunity brokers and enablers among university students?", *International Entrepreneurship and Management Journal*, Vol. 13, No. 1, pp. 97–111.

Taylor, L. (2020). "of Larry Page and Sergey Brin, who created Google during their Ph.D. studies at Stanford and Jerry Yang, who created Yahoo! in university". Available at: www.cnbc.com/2020/07/29/google-to-instagram-stanford-alumni-that-founded-notable-companies.html

Wilson, K. (2008) " Chapter 5: Entrepreneurship Education in Europe". OECD, 2008, Available at SSRN: https://ssrn.com/abstract=1392369

2 Setting entrepreneurship skill to foster venture building

2.1 The relevance of entrepreneurship education

Entrepreneurship education is defined as the process of equipping individuals with the concepts, skills, and abilities necessary for entrepreneurship to recognize opportunities that others have overlooked and to have the self-confidence to act where others have hesitated (Zhang et al., 2014). Higher education is seen as a factor that leads young people to have an entrepreneurial awareness and to choose an entrepreneurial career pat. In fact, the educational context can significantly contribute to the development of essential knowledge and skills that young entrepreneurs need to succeed in their business ventures, reducing the risk of failure (Gabrielsson et al., 2020). For example, Al-Omar et al. (2024) shows how entrepreneurship education acts on intention through the development of creative capacities, entrepreneurial skills, and technical knowledge that are necessary to start a new business venture and face the job market though a flexible approach to identify opportunities and take risks, work in teams, and better equipped to solve problems. Entrepreneurship education allows not only students to start their own business, but more importantly it trains their entrepreneurial mindset (Rippa et al., 2023) and increase their flexibility in their career choice and thus to better succeed in their job intents even in challenging environments, especially those characterized by economic instability (Passavanti et al., 2023).

Entrepreneurship education can have a positive impact on students' intrinsic motivation. In fact, it can encourage students to turn their entrepreneurial intentions into concrete actions. Hence, motivated and well-prepared students who have undergone entrepreneurship training programs are more likely to initiate new ventures (e.g. Stamboulis

DOI: 10.4324/9781003607649-3

and Barlas, 2014; Wright et al., 2017). To this point, the metastudy provided by Martínez-Gregorio et al., (2021) shows that entrepreneurial education impact on entrepreneurial intent is significant and applies also to students that have not exhibited prior interest in entrepreneurship.

This impact was recently confirmed by the study of Llorente Potillo et al. (2024) which measured the entrepreneurial intention of a group of students from the University of Menterrey who were exposed to entrepreneurship courses and showed how hands-on activities and direct engagement between teachers and students, as well as the creation of a personalized learning environment, increased students' self-confidence, and thus their intention to become entrepreneurs.

Entrepreneurial education proves to be particularly relevant in rural settings, as highlighted by Moore and Breece (2023) who showed how entrepreneurship courses made possible the development of an entrepreneurial mindset, by increasing the creation of sustainable ecosystems and incentivizing the design of new entrepreneurial ventures among students.

2.2 The role of universities in entrepreneurship education

Universities are seen as facilitators of student entrepreneurship through student education, as they provide an environment apt to transfer to individuals with specific, valuable knowledge that can leverage entrepreneurship projects and can positively influence the project and ideas of students involved in nascent entrepreneurship (Leiva et al., 2023). This is confirmed by the GEM Adult Population Survey 2021 which evidenced that globally, on average, the level of total early-stage Entrepreneurial Activity (TEA) for graduates is higher than for nongraduate. This is consistent with the new role of universities in society and the economy (Etzkowitz and Leydesdorff, 2000) which goes beyond their traditional focus on research and knowledge transfer (Wright, 2014). Moreover, the literature identifies the need to adopt new paradigms in the teaching of entrepreneurship that go beyond the traditional models that are related to theoretical learning, towards the implementation of experiential models (learning "for"), that are based on the acquisition of knowledge that can be used in different contexts. It is a novel approach that works on the development of the student's entrepreneurial mindset and soft skills such as creativity, critical, and analytical thinking (Wahid et al., 2017), thus forming competencies that aim to give students the ability to face the uncertainty, complexity, and dynamics of the current labor market (Perić et al., 2020). Universities are called upon to create safe environments where students can learn how to face challenges and recognize opportunities in complex and evolving scenarios. This imply for Universities to experiment new teaching strategies to enhance entrepreneurial skills (Cope, 2003) that are more inquiry-oriented, that enhance the peer-to-peer learning and that are based on continuous feedback (Grigg, 2021).

Universities are also called upon to interact with the entrepreneurial ecosystems, to promote the contamination between business and academia, through the active involvement of students in business projects to create an effective entrepreneurial learning experience for the participants (Karanassios et al., 2006), by modelling strong links between theory and practice and enhance student contact with the local and global business world. Among the activities that can be organized to foster entrepreneurship, studies have focused on the relevance of experiential education tools such as projects, simulations, roleplaying, guest lecturers, community work, and extracurricular activities (Lesinskis et al., 2021; Perić et al., 2020). Such relational activities can contribute to the creation of communities of practices within universities, which can leverage the social network and the social capital (Jones, 2022). However, scholars pointed out that alongside soft skills, universities are called upon to emphasize entrepreneurial and managerial skills (Vera and Vicent, 2024), together with technological skills (such as coding and digital competences) as they are recognized as having a positive a significant influence on students' entrepreneurial engagement and student entrepreneurial intent (Sansone et al., 2024).

Scholars also recall the importance of University infrastructures as an element that acts as a facilitator of the processes of entrepreneurial learning effectiveness. The external environment of universities, in addition to the construction of courses, should be able to promote entrepreneurship. A particular strength is to promote, through extracurricular activities, an innovative orientation through technological infrastructure such as e-learning platforms, product modeling tools (such as 3D systems), and experimental laboratories, or even automated digital software for evaluating the business ideas (Lesinskis et al., 2021). These are complemented by the ability of universities to foster student mobility. In fact, overseas travel and academic exchanges are a source for increasing entrepreneurial culture. Studies also emphasize the relevance of providing students with incentives through prizes and hackathons that guide the development of startup ideas and projects (Slišāne et al., 2021).

Moreover, it is relevant to design programs that are individualized and allow active interaction between instructors and students as a factor in increasing self-efficacy (Chen, 2013). In this regard, studies emphasize the relevance of integrated entrepreneurial mentoring within entrepreneurship programs (Hadjichristodoulou et al., 2020), as it is able to create relationships that have a positive impact on entrepreneurial identity and venture progress, acting on the student's network and ability to cope with difficulties along the start-up journey (Ahsan et al., 2018).

However, training models should not be designed in a standardized way, but should be adapted to the specific context in which they are implemented. Hence, it is important that they are tailored to the regional needs and cultural characteristics of the context where they are initiated (Mets et al., 2021).

2.3 Setting entrepreneurship education in the EU

In Europe, entrepreneurship education has established as an important lever to address societal and economic challenges and effective mean to counteract youth unemployment.[1] This was recently recalled by Mario Draghi as part of his report on the future of European competitiveness, emphasizing how entrepreneurship is one of the key competencies for boosting EU competitiveness and should be integrated into curricula.[2]

While entrepreneurship is now fully recognized as a lever for promoting innovation and European competitiveness and as a factor in strengthening social cohesion in the European space;[3] however, its formal recognition and enhancement in the EU has been gradual and linked to external shocks that have involved the EU during the 2000s.

2.3.1 Early recognition of the role of entrepreneurial mindset

The relevance of entrepreneurship education within the European space was first stated in 2006, as part of the Oslo Agenda for Entrepreneurship Education in Europe. This document has been promoted in lights of the Conference on "Entrepreneurship Education in Europe: Fostering Entrepreneurial Mindsets through Education and Learning" held in Oslo on 26–27 October 2006. The Conference was a follow-up to the

Communication titled "Fostering Entrepreneurial Mindsets through Education and Learning"[4] adopted by the Commission with the aim to set guidelines at European and national level to promote entrepreneurship at all level of education, by fostering partnerships among private and public stakeholders.[5]

Furthermore, the Council adopted the recommendation on "Key Competences for Lifelong Learning",[6] that reaffirmed the need to equip young people with the necessary key competences and improve educational attainment levels in order to create a future-oriented education system capable of supporting integration into the world of work, thereby fostering social cohesion and enabling citizens to acquire more flexible skills. The recommendation recognizes this will give them increased fulfilment and greater capacity to adapt to rapidly changing economic and social contexts to achieve dynamic models of employability consistent with the development of a knowledge-based society. The Council's document set forth eight key competences shown in Table 2.1 that are intertwined and support each other, to leverage positive outcome of European citizens in society. These imply the development of relevant soft skills, such as such as critical thinking, problem solving, team work, communication and negotiation skills, analytical skills, creativity, and intercultural skills, including the entrepreneurship competence.

According to the Council's Recommendation, entrepreneurship means to show capacity to turn opportunities and ideas into cultural, social, or financial value. The competence is described as being the results of showing creativity, critical thinking, and problem solving, and of the ability to take initiative resilience, and to work with others (Table 2.2).

Table 2.1 Reference framework of key competences for lifelong learning

Literacy competence
Multilingual competence
Mathematical competence and competence in science, technology and engineering
Digital competence
Personal, social and learning to learn competence
Citizenship competence
Entrepreneurship competence
Cultural awareness and expression competence

Source: Council recommendation "Key Competences for Lifelong Learning".

Table 2.2 Entrepreneurship competence

Area	*Essential knowledge, skills and attitudes related to this competence*
Entrepreneurship process	"Entrepreneurship competence requires knowing that there are different contexts and opportunities for turning ideas into action in personal, social and professional activities, and an understanding of how these arise. Individuals should know and understand approaches to planning and management of projects, which include both processes and resources. They should have an understanding of economics and the social and economic opportunities and challenges facing an employer, organisation or society. They should also be aware of ethical principles and challenges of sustainable development and have self-awareness of their own strengths and weaknesses".
Entrepreneurship skills	"Entrepreneurial skills are founded on creativity which includes imagination, strategic thinking and problem-solving, and critical and constructive reflection within evolving creative processes and innovation. They include the ability to work both as an individual and collaboratively in teams, to mobilize resources (people and things) and to sustain activity. This includes the ability to make financial decisions relating to cost and value. The ability to effectively communicate and negotiate with others, and to cope with uncertainty, ambiguity and risk as part of making informed decisions is essential".
Entrepreneurial mindset	"An entrepreneurial attitude is characterised by a sense of initiative and agency, pro-activity, being forward-looking, courage and perseverance in achieving objectives. It includes a desire to motivate others and value their ideas, empathy and taking care of people and the world, and accepting responsibility taking ethical approaches throughout the process".

Source: Council recommendation "Key Competences for Lifelong Learning".

2.3.2 The financial crisis and the role of young entrepreneurship

A further advance towards the recognition of the key role of entrepreneurial education at the European level was made in the aftermath of the global financial crisis of 2008 and the subsequent debt crisis of

2011 that hit the EU. The financial crisis of 2008 caused the increase in unemployment levels, which exceeded 25% in some EU member countries such as Spain, and Greece and was particularly high for young people.[7] In this context, the EU further recognized entrepreneurship as one of the key skills capable of counteracting the effects of the financial crisis, especially among younger segments of the population, promoting self-employment as a tool to overcome the youth unemployment crisis.

In 2009, in the aftermath of the Great recession, the EU published the "EU Strategy for Youth – Investing and Empowering",[8] that was considered as a coordination tool to address the needs of EU young people.

In the Communication, the importance of investing in entrepreneurship education is fully recognized as a means to overcome the structural challenges to competitiveness and growth and counteract the negative effect of the economic downturn on the labor market, especially on youth unemployment, by leveraging the ability of young individual to find opportunities, take risks, work in teams and solve problems.

In this context, the Commission adopted the Communication "Rethinking Education: Investing in skills for better socio-economic outcomes"[9] where it points to the need to train individuals by transferring the skills that the world of work will require in future. This would imply that the educational system of the European Member states should aim to equip individuals with 21st century skills, which are not only technical but also include transversal skills. Among the transversal skills, a particular role is assigned to entrepreneurial skills. By the Commission, entrepreneurial skills are considered as a key 'soft' competences for all, which should therefore be promoted at all levels of education (from primary school to university). Moreover, entrepreneurial skills are key to accelerate new business creation and the process of integrating young people into the labor market through self-employability.

For the first time, in its communication, the European Commission recalls the importance of building new educational models, especially at University level, to promote entrepreneurial skills through new and creative ways of teaching and learning. According to the Commission, this should include knowledge about how to set up a business as a career choice by adopting new pedagogical approaches through real-world experience, problem-based learning, and business connections.

More importantly, the European Commission reaffirms the concept of universality of entrepreneurial education, establishing that all young people should benefit from at least one practical entrepreneurial experience before leaving compulsory schooling.

The 2012 Communication on "Rethinking Education" was followed by the "Entrepreneurship 2020 Action Plan", presented by the Commission in January 2013.[10] The Action Plan further recognized entrepreneurship as a key driver to strengthen employability and initiate a behavioral change to develop a culture of innovation that should be inclusive and aimed at creating businesses and value for society. In this context, entrepreneurship education is a lever to promote entrepreneurial venture; consequently, the EU should encourage the introduction of entrepreneurship as a skill to be taught at all levels of education by means of informal or nonformal learning.

However, the plan recalls that meeting the objective of setting sustainable entrepreneurship would require the European Union to create the conditions for capacity building in entrepreneurship by setting up new policy frameworks. These should be aimed not only to facilitate business creation and the development of new ideas but also to foster the dissemination of a positive culture of doing business.[11]

2.4 The EU framework for entrepreneurial competences—EntreComp

Relevant for the development of agreed guidelines on entrepreneurship education within the EU common market is "The New Skills Agenda for Europe" plan and the "Recommendation on key competences for lifelong learning"[12] launched, respectively, in 2016 and 2018. The New Skills Agenda for Europe" action plan aimed to foster cooperation between states and support from EU institutions for state-led initiatives to develop individuals' resilience to rapidly changing environments through the development of key skills and competences. The document assigns a key role to entrepreneurship support programs and emphasizes that entrepreneurship should aim to promote an entrepreneurial and innovation mindset, including the creation of conditions conducive to the development of practical entrepreneurial experience. The "Recommendation on key competences for lifelong learning"[13] further reinforces the need to work on competences as a means to ensure inclusion and access to job opportunities to support adequate living standards and the resilience of the EU in the face of ongoing external changes and to create a society that shows increased mobility and digital competences. Among the key competences for lifelong learning,[14] the Recommendation also inserts the "entrepreneurship competence". The recommendation further emphasizes the inherently agentic nature of entrepreneurship, based on a deep understanding of the context and the ability to act proactively within it.

Entrepreneurs are conceived as agents of change, capable of generating innovation by identifying and developing new opportunities. From the European Union's point of view, promoting entrepreneurship would require a structured set of skills that constitute the entrepreneurial mindset, to include the ethical dimension. This aspect is in line with the acknowledgement, both by the EU and in the academic literature, of the crucial role of entrepreneurial skills as a driver for the achievement of the sustainable development goals (SDGs). The Recommendation further stresses the importance of fostering entrepreneurial skills such as creativity and sense of initiative, especially among young people, by promoting opportunities for young students to undertake at least one practical entrepreneurial experience during their school education.

2.4.1 The raise of the EntreComp model

According to the European Commission, the basic competences in the field of entrepreneurship are articulated in different but interrelated dimensions. At the core is the ability to plan and manage projects, both processes and resources, accompanied by a solid understanding of the economic mechanisms and socioeconomic dynamics that influence organizations and society. This foundation is integrated with an awareness of ethical principles and the challenges of sustainable development, as well as a deep self-awareness of one's own potential and limitations. Creativity emerges as a transversal element, manifested through imagination, strategic thinking, and problem solving, supported by critical and constructive reflection in creative and innovative processes.

These skills are expressed at both individual and collective levels; indeed, the EU considers the ability to work effectively in a team, mobilize human and material resources, and manage financial aspects to be paramount for the entrepreneur. In addition, managing the financial aspects of entrepreneurial ventures, together with an awareness of the cost–benefit ratio, are among the skills that characterize the entrepreneurial mindset. The ability to communicate effectively, negotiate, and manage situations of uncertainty and risk in the decision-making process are also fundamental.

To support the development of these skills, the EU calls for the implementation of innovative educational approaches that integrate digital technologies while strengthening support for teachers and families in the learning process. Particular attention is paid to the need to develop harmonized models for skills assessment between Member States and consolidate tools to support continuous training, thus creating a coherent and sustainable educational ecosystem for entrepreneurial development in the European Union.

The European declarations were followed by work on systematizing entrepreneurial competencies on the part of the EU, culminating in the development of the Entrepreneurship Competence Framework (EntreComp). The framework seeks to fill a gap about the harmonization of lifelong competencies recognized as key to supporting the activation of an entrepreneurial mindset and facilitating business venturing within the European common market. The EU competency model was developed by the Joint Research Centre, in partnership with DG Employment, Social Affairs and Inclusion, through a mixed methodology based on the analysis of scientific and grey literature review, in-depth interviews, and case studies. The process included a consultation phase involving multiple stakeholders (Bacigalupo et al. 2016).

Three following key areas of competences in the field of entrepreneurship were identified:

1) Ideas and opportunities
2) Resources
3) Action

Each of these three dimensions was subdivided into five distinct competences, which were considered as interrelated and key to the effectiveness of entrepreneurial learning. Each of the five competences is further linked to a set of five key competences, as shown in Figure 2.1. The sub competences are linked to a list of 442 learning outcomes.

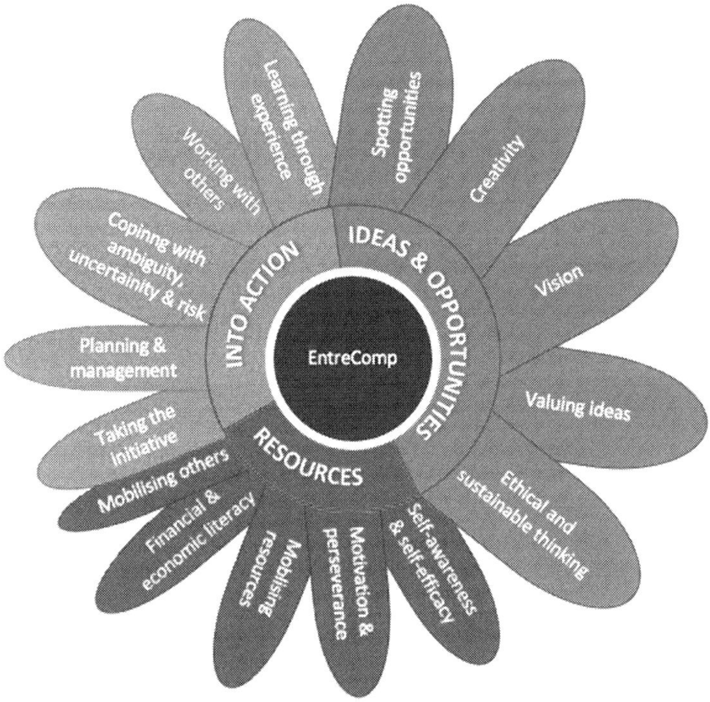

Figure 2.1 The EntreComp competency model.

2.4.2 The evaluation of EntreComp model

The ability to achieve learning objectives with EntreComp is articulated through two fundamental and interrelated dimensions. The first concerns the process of transforming opportunities and ideas into value-creating initiatives and the progressive development of autonomy and responsibility. The second relates to enhancing the ability to create value in contexts of increasing complexity, ranging from predictable situations to dynamic and complex, ever-changing environments.

Furthermore, the EntreComp framework establishes a correlation between specific learning objectives and subject areas. These are structured into eight evolutionary stages. These stages follow a progression from basic, intermediate, and advanced to mastery, with each stage further divided into two distinct phases. At the basic level, the individual learns to create entrepreneurial value with the guidance and support of others. At the intermediate level, there is increasing autonomy in the creation of entrepreneurial value. The advanced level focuses on building the ability to translate concepts into concrete actions, while the mastery level is characterized by the production of value that can have a significant impact on the industry.

The effectiveness of EntreComp for entrepreneurial development in the European Union has been widely recognized in numerous studies (Grigg, 2021; Seikkula-Leino et al., 2021), and EntreComp has emerged as a model that has been validated by several subsequent researches. Of particular importance is the study by Armuña et al. (2020) who applied the model to explore the relationship between entrepreneurial skills and entrepreneurial intention (EI) in a sample of potential STEM entrepreneurs. Floris and Pillitu (2019) on the other hand, implemented the framework as a reference pedagogical model for entrepreneurial education programs in Italy. Further works contributed to the validation of the model by applying the EntreComp framework in a university setting, using it as a tool to compare the entrepreneurial competences of different groups of students (Czyzewska and Mroczek, 2020).

A relevant in-depth comparative analysis was carried out by Gianesini et al. (2018) who compared EntreComp with three competing models and taxonomies of pre-existing entrepreneurial competences, namely the 13 Competencies model and the Great Eight model. Their research highlighted the uniqueness of EntreComp in its ability to identify, directly or indirectly, key entrepreneurial competencies related to students' entrepreneurial mindset. In this study, the authors show that Ideas & Opportunities, found in EnteComp, is a predictive dimension of entrepreneurship and guides students' entrepreneurial intention. Furthermore, it is recognized that the EntreComp model, compared to other models, proposes an articulation of competences that is more in line with the aspects that characterize entrepreneurship competences: ideas (i.e. creativity, opportunity, and feasibility), to synthesize the resources that constitute a stimulus to entrepreneurship (i.e. personal, human capital, economic) and incentives and barriers to the ability of individuals to give shape to ideas by transforming them into a new venture (i.e. initiative, management, planning, adaptation; Figure 2.2).

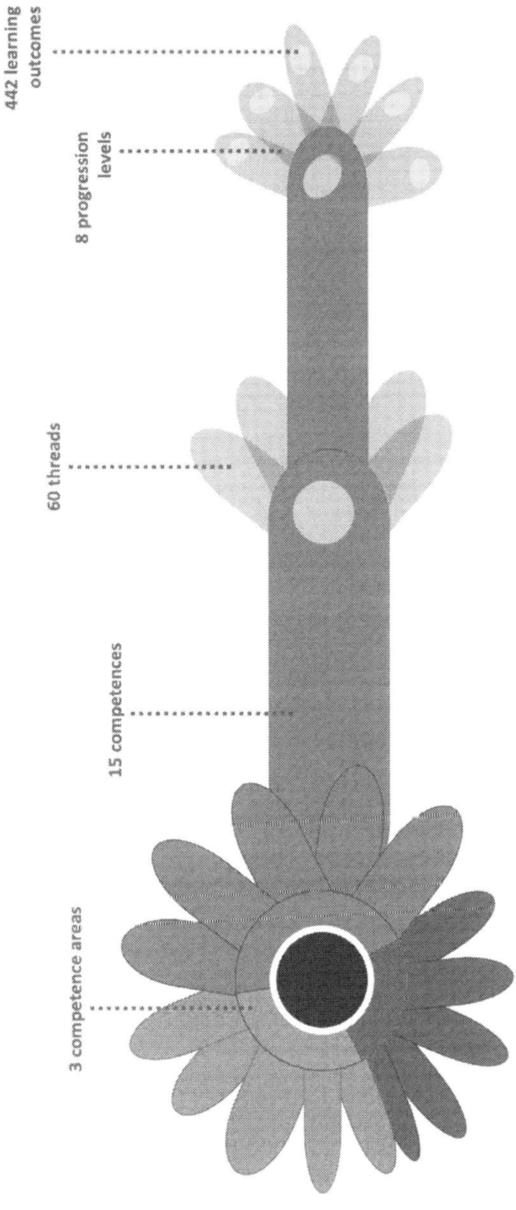

Figure 2.2 The competence structure in EntreComp.

2.5 COVID-19 and the role of entrepreneurship education in the EU

The COVID-19 pandemic and subsequent economic constraints led to a deep global crisis that also involved the EU. In 2020, the European Union experienced a 6.1% fall in EU real GDP. This fall was even more severe than during financial crisis on 2008–2009[15]—when the EU's overall GDP fell by 4%.

During the pandemic, the industrial production reached the levels of the 1990s with unemployment peaking at 10% of the working population, approximately 23 million people, and 1.2 million jobs. In order to overcome this crisis, in 2020, the EU adopted the "Next Generation EU" instrument, a set of measures to stimulate Europe's recovery totaling 2.018 trillion euros. Next generation EU also represented a strategy to project Europe into the future, showing proactivity in face of the crisis to design a smarter, more sustainable, and inclusive Europe. The crisis linked to the COVID-19 pandemic also enhanced the vulnerability of younger generations. Youth unemployment reached 13.3% in 2020 and stood at 13% in 2021, accounting for 5 million unemployed young people aged 15–29. This limited the capabilities of young adults to make the transition from education to work and forced young people to rethink their plans for independence.[16]

2.5.1 Inclusion policies generation and the role of entrepreneurship

The severity of the COVID-19 crisis and subsequent economic constraints led to a surge in the NEETs population, reaching 13.8% in 2020, primarily due to employment losses and reduced access to educational and training opportunities for youth. Since 2021, however, there has been a consistent downward trend in the NEET's[17] rate, culminating in a historic minimum of 11.2% in 2023.

In this setting, the EU reinforced the measures planned for young people, with a focus on NEETs, through the strengthening of the initiative "Supporting youth employment: a bridge to work for the next generation", with the aim of "building a bridge to work for the next generation" and "facilitating the acquisition of the skills, training and education needed to adapt to a rapidly changing environment".

The focus on NEETs follows the European Commission's aim to support networks of potential entrepreneurs by disseminating good practice and strengthening links with the business world, useful for creating role models, as well as incubators and other local support services for start-ups. In particular, the Commission aims to provide opportunities for specific categories of missing entrepreneurs, such as young women and other discriminated or vulnerable groups, foster sustainable entrepreneurship at national and local levels, and reintegrate people excluded from the labor market with a more positive social impact.

2.5.2 The YEPA initiative

Recognizing the value of networks for entrepreneurship and the need to create a common ecosystemic approach to the dissemination of entrepreneurial skills as a lever of EU development, in 2023 the European Commission jointly with OECD launched the Youth Entrepreneurship Policy Academy (YEPA) initiative, a European Entrepreneurial Learning Policy Network with 150 participants, including policymakers, youth entrepreneurship networks and organizations, social entrepreneurship networks, program managers, and researchers. YEPA aims to strengthen youth entrepreneurship policies and programs across Europe by increasing knowledge about the barriers young people face in entrepreneurship and facilitating exchange between policymakers, young entrepreneurs, and experts about the efficacy of entrepreneurship policies.[18]

The YEPA initiative organizes workshops, discussion notes, and reports, which are intended to be a moment of active discussion among network members on the future of young entrepreneurship.

2.6 Conclusions

The chapter provides an overview of the main theories related to entrepreneurship education, with particular reference to the European experience. By reconstructing the steps that led to the affirmation of the relevance of entrepreneurship education within the European Union, the chapter presents the areas of greatest focus for the EU with regard to the content of entrepreneurship education, presenting EntreComp and its feature. Furthermore, the work summarizes recent developments in entrepreneurship education in Europe, focusing mainly on the missing entrepreneurs to highlight how the current EU perspective is to address issues related to entrepreneurship education by using the concept of networks between stakeholders to raise awareness and spread good practices.

Notes

1 European Commission (2013). Reigniting the entrepreneurial spirit in Europe.
European Commission. (2014). Thematic working group on entrepreneurship education. Available at: https://ec.europa.eu/assets/eac/education/experts-groups/2011-2013/key/entrepreneurship-report-2014_en.pdf
2 Mario Draghi (2024), *The future of European competitiveness report*. September 2024.
3 Council Recommendation of 22 May 2018 on key competences Framework.
4 COM(2006) 33 final, available at: https://eur-lex.europa.eu/LexUriServ/LexUriServ.do?uri=COM%3A2006%3A0033%3AFIN%3AEN%3APDF
5 COM(2006) 33 final.
6 2018/C 189/01, available at: https://eur-lex.europa.eu/legal-content/EN/TXT/?uri=uriserv:OJ.C_.2018.189.01.0001.01.ENG&toc=OJ:C:2018:189:TOC
7 European Central Bank (2014), "The impact of the economic crisis on euro area labour marKets". ECB Monthly Bulletin, October 2014. Available at: www.ecb.europa.eu/pub/pdf/other/art1_mb201410_pp49-68.en.pdf
8 An EU Strategy for Youth – Investing and Empowering a renewed open method of coordination to address youth challenges and opportunities. COM(2009) 200 final. Available at: https://eur-lex.europa.eu/LexUriServ/LexUriServ.do?uri=COM:2009:0200:FIN:EN:PDF
9 COM/2012/0669 final.
10 COM (2012) 795 final.
11 European Parliament (2013), "Promoting entrepreneurship through education".
12 2018/C 189/01.
13 2018/C 189/01.
14 2018/C 189/01.
15 CEPR, "The EU economy after COVID-19: Implications for economic governance". Available at: https://cepr.org/voxeu/columns/eu-economy-after-covid-19-implications-economic-governance
16 Eurofound (2021), *Impact of COVID-19 on young people in the EU*, Publications Office of the European Union, Luxembourg.
17 NEET is an acronym referring to young persons not engaged in education, employment, or training. This includes young people aged between 15 and 29 in the EU.
18 Detailed Information about the YEPA initiative are available at: https://yepa-hub.org/why-yepa/

References

Ahsan, M., Zheng, C., DeNoble, A. and Musteen, M. (2018). "From student to entrepreneur: How mentorships and affect influence student venture launch", *Journal of Small Business Management*, Vol. 56, No. 1, pp. 76–102.

Al-Omar, S., Alalawneh, A. and Harb, A. (2024). "The impact of entrepreneurship education on entrepreneurial intention: The moderating role of perceived governmental support", *Education + Training*, Vol. 66, No. 7, pp. 777–800.

Armuña, C., Ramos, S., Juan, J., Feijóo, C. and Arenal, A. (2020). "From stand-up to start-up: Exploring entrepreneurship competences and STEM women's intention", *International Entrepreneurship and Management Journal*, Vol. 16 No. 1, pp. 69–92.

Bacigalupo M, Kampylis P, Punie Y and Van Den Brande L. (2016). "EntreComp: The Entrepreneurship Competence Framework". Luxembourg (Luxembourg): Publications Office of the European Union; 2016. JRC101581

Chen, L. (2013). "IT entrepreneurial intention among college students: An empirical study," *Journal of Information Systems Education*, Vol. 24, No. 3, pp. 233–244. https://aisel.aisnet.org/jise/vol24/iss3/8

Cope, J. (2003). "Entrepreneurial learning and critical reflection: Discontinuous events as triggers for 'Higher-level' learning", *Management Learning*, Vol. 34, No. 4, pp. 429–450.

Czyzewska, M. and Mroczek, T. (2020). "Data mining in entrepreneurial competencies diagnosis", *Education Sciences*, Vol. 10(8) 196, pp. 1–27 https://doi.org/10.3390/educsci10080196

Etzkowitz, H. and Leydesdorff, L. (2000). "The dynamics of innovation: From National Systems and 'Mode 2' to a Triple Helix of university–industry–government relations", *Research Policy*, Vol. 29 No. 2, pp. 109–123.

Floris, M. and Pillitu, D. (2019). "Improving entrepreneurship education in primary schools: A pioneer project", *International Journal of Educational Management*, Vol. 33, No. 6, pp. 1148–1169.

Gabrielsson, J., Hägg, G., Landström, H. and Politis, D. (2020). "Connecting the past with the present: The development of research on pedagogy in entrepreneurial education", *Education + Training*, Vol. 62, No. 9, pp. 1061–1086.

Gianesini, G., Cubico, S., Favretto, G. and Leitão, J.C. (2018). "Entrepreneurial competences: Comparing and contrasting models and ttaxonomies", In *Entrepreneurship and the Industry Life Cycle*, pp. 13–32.

Grigg, R. (2021). "EntreCompEdu, a professional development framework for entrepreneurial education", *Education and Training*, Vol. 63, No. 7–8, pp. 1058–1072.

Hadjichristodoulou, V., Varnava Marouchou, D., Konis, E. and Mihai Yiannaki, S. (2020). "The success of STEM graduates in entrepreneurship training: A European case study", *Global Business and Economics Review*, Vol. 22, No. 1/2, p. 198.

Jones, O. (2022). "Academic engagement with small business and entrepreneurship: Towards a landscape of practice", *Industry and Higher Education*, Vol. 36, No. 3, pp. 279–293.

Karanassios, N., Pazarskis, M., Mitsopoulos, K. and Christodoulou, P. (2006). "EU strategies to encourage youth entrepreneurship: Evidence from higher education in Greece", *Industry and Higher Education*, Vol. 20, No. 1, pp. 43–50.

Leiva, J.C., Mora-Esquivel, R. and Solís, M. (2023). "Nascent entrepreneurship in university students: The role of the context", *Venture Capital*, Vol. 25, No. 3, pp. 255–284.

Lesinskis, K., Mavlutova, I., Peiseniece, L., Hermanis, J., Peiseniece, E. and Pokatayeva, O. (2021). "Modern business teaching: The sable labor market provision for the emerging generations", *Estudios de Economia Aplicada*, Vol. 39, No 5, pp. 1–7 https://doi.org/10.25115/eea.v39i5.5202

Martínez-Gregorio, S., Badenes-Ribera, L. and Oliver, A. (2021). "Effect of entrepreneurship education on entrepreneurship intention and related outcomes in educational contexts: A meta-analysis", *International Journal of Management Education*, Vol. 19, No. 3, 100545.

Mets, T., Holbrook, J. and Läänelaid, S. (2021). "Entrepreneurship education challenges for green transformation", *Administrative Sciences*, Vol. 11, No. 1. 15, pp. 1–15.

Moore, S. and Breece, D.D. (2023). "Unleashing entrepreneurial opportunities and education: Impact of an innovation design lab", *Entrepreneurship Education and Pedagogy*, Vol. 7, No. 3, pp. 377–389.

No, I., Llorente-portillo, C., Dobson, J.A., Omari, N.K. and Gómez-urquijo, L. (2024). "Entrepreneurial intention development: The contribution of specialized entrepreneurship academic programs", *Tuning Journal of Higher Education*, Vol. 11, No. pp. 637–669.

Passavanti, C., Ponsiglione, C., Primario, S. and Rippa, P. (2023). "The evolution of student entrepreneurship: State of the art and emerging research direction", *International Journal of Management Education*, Vol. 21, No. 2, 100820.

Perić, J., Oberman Peterka, S. and Getoš, Ž. (2020). "The role of vocational education in developing entrepreneurial competences of students", *Ekonomski Pregled*, Vol. 71, No. 5, pp. 463–492.

Rippa, P., Ferruzzi, G., Holienka, M., Capaldo, G. and Coduras, A. (2023). "What drives university engineering students to become entrepreneurs? Finding different recipes using a configuration approach", *Journal of Small Business Management*, Vol. 61, No. 2, pp. 353–383.

Sansone, G., Ghezzi, A., Landoni, P. and Rangone, A. (2024). "Students' entrepreneurial engagement and student entrepreneurship: Do coding and digital skills matter?", *IEEE Transactions on Engineering Management*, Vol. 71, No. March, pp. 5733–5743.

Seikkula-Leino, J., Salomaa, M., Jónsdóttir, S.R., McCallum, E. and Israel, H. (2021). "Eu policies driving entrepreneurial competences—Reflections from the case of entrecomp", *Sustainability (Switzerland)*, Vol. 13, No. 15, pp. 1–21 https://doi.org/10.3390/su13158178

Slišāne, A., Lāma, G. and Rubene, Z. (2021). "Self-assessment of the entrepreneurial competence of teacher education students in the remote study process", *Sustainability (Switzerland)*, Vol. 13, No. 11., pp. 1–14. https://doi.org/10.3390/su13116424

Stamboulis, Y. and Barlas, A. (2014). "Entrepreneurship education impact on student attitudes", *International Journal of Management Education*, Vol. 12, No. 3, pp. 365–373.

Vera, M. and Vicent, P. (2024). "The competence of digital entrepreneurship in education: Analysis of the perception of university students", *Intangible Capital*, Vol. 20, p. 376.

Wahid, N.A., Abd Aziz, N.N. and Halim, R.A. (2017). "Networking and innovation performance of micro-enterprises in Malaysia: The moderating effects of geographical location", *Pertanika Journal of Social Sciences and Humanities*, Vol. 25, No. S, pp. 277–287.

Wright, M. (2014). "Academic entrepreneurship, technology transfer and society: Where next?", *Journal of Technology Transfer*, Vol. 39, No. 3, pp. 322–334.

Wright, M., Siegel, D.S. and Mustar, P. (2017). "An emerging ecosystem for student start-ups", *Journal of Technology Transfer*, Vol. 42, No. 4, pp. 909–922.

Zhang, Y., Duysters, G. and Cloodt, M. (2014). "The role of entrepreneurship education as a predictor of university students' entrepreneurial intention", *International Entrepreneurship and Management Journal*, Vol. 10, No. 3, pp. 623–641.

3 Framing a European model of entrepreneurship education

Contributors: Paola Belingheri and Christian Lechner from LUISS

3.1 European universities and the creation of new ventures

Educational factors, especially when it comes to entrepreneurship education, have proven to significantly influence student attitudes and intentions towards entrepreneurship (Maheshwari et al., 2022). Specifically, Chaudhary (2017) shows how being exposed to knowledge that can influence one's propensity to become an entrepreneur is high among students from business schools where students appear to be more entrepreneurially inclined than students taking other courses. The availability of knowledge resources about entrepreneurship is also high among students with experience and among those who have already started their own businesses (Bergmann et al., 2014).

In Europe, universities seem to have taken a leading role in helping young people along the entrepreneurship path, with activities and university courses focused on entrepreneurship (Wilson, 2008), thus going beyond teaching and research activities to show active involvement in society (Forliano et al., 2021) and making a significant contribution to accelerating the transfer of research and development (R&D) knowledge and innovation to the broader business community as well as stimulating economic growth (Sá and Pinho, 2019).

This transformation has led to the creation of entrepreneurial universities as new models of learning institutions that include knowledge management activities. In addition to teaching entrepreneurship, entrepreneurial universities get involved in technology transfer, regional development, and stakeholder engagement initiatives, as well as actions that prioritize the creation of ties to industry, society, and government (López-Núñez et al., 2021).

DOI: 10.4324/9781003607649-4

The transformation of the role of universities and their centrality in the processes of creating new businesses in Europe has been accelerated by the so-called Bologna Process.[1] The Bologna Process has gradually harmonized and simplified higher education systems in participating countries while also strengthening qualification frameworks at the European level (Kushnir, 2016). This path has not only led to the establishment of a system of comparable degrees at the European level, but has also strengthened the sharing of common views and values in higher education—strengthening cross-border cooperation among universities and increasing the mobility of researchers, teachers, and administrative and technical staff, thereby accelerating the processes of generating new knowledge at the European level in the university sphere. Moreover, the latest communiqué from the Ministerial Conference of the European Higher Education Area[2] emphasizes the need to further strengthen the innovation and entrepreneurial capacities of universities in response to the new challenges of digitalization and in accordance with the importance of achieving the sustainable development goals (SDGs) and the green transition.

Data show the ever-increasing ability of European universities to act as accelerators in the creation of new ventures, moving closer to the European model. The Redstone University Start-up Index 2024[3] shows that European universities could generate more than 157,000 additional start-ups over the next 10 years and could contribute to the creation of new jobs and to the increase of the national GDP. However, differences exist among European regions and in the ability of local universities to act as drivers for the creation of new ventures.

Actually, the study shows that France, Spain, the UK, Germany, the Netherlands, Sweden, and Italy are the countries with the highest potential for start-up creation and with the greatest potential economic impact, while countries such as Malta, Cyprus, and Croatia have limited capacity (Table 3.1).

Such regional disparities were also highlighted by a study focused on Europe's top schools ranked by start-up founders, conducted by Pitchbook in 2023.[4] The report shows that the majority of European graduate student founders come from universities located in the UK, with 3,957 companies founded by UK university graduates in 2021. The University of Cambridge, University of Oxford, and Imperial College London are at the top of the rankings (Figure 3.1). This achievement can be attributed to the thriving entrepreneurial ecosystem in the UK and the proactive approach of its universities, which

Table 3.1 Potential opportunities from startup universities (first ranked)

Country	*# Startups*	*# Jobs*	*Equity value (in €Bn)*
England	32.264	1.262.074	662.6
Germany	25.929	1.014.290	539.5
France	16.688	652.804	365.7
Netherlands	10.932	427.623	224.5
Spain	10.427	407.869	214.1
Sweden	8.606	336.629	176.7
Italy	7.494	293.152	153.9
Switzerland	6.013	235.198	123.5
Belgium	5.936	232.198	121.9
Denmark	4.702	183.949	96.6

Source: Redstone.

have been at the forefront in terms of encouraging and mentoring students in their entrepreneurial pursuits. Sweden has also made significant strides in this arena, with 962 start-ups founded by graduate students from listed universities financed by venture capital firms (VC), from Jan 2013 to September 2023. France and the Netherlands follow closely behind, with 829 and 701 companies, respectively, founded by graduate students from the listed universities financed by VC. Next in line are Denmark, Switzerland, Germany, Finland, and Belgium, with, respectively, 390, 369, 238, 228, and 276 companies founded by graduate students from their listed universities. Top universities in other European countries are also making remarkable progress in nurturing student entrepreneurship.

By looking at the distribution of student start-ups across major cities,[5] what emerges is that cities with the highest university budgets (top 15) have the highest number of start-ups funded by graduate students. The cities with the highest concentration of student start-ups are those with innovation ecosystems, such as Barcelona, Paris, Milan, and London.

3.2 Mapping entrepreneurship education in Europe

Available reports and statistics about student entrepreneurship in Europe show that it is becoming an increasingly central theme in European higher education, with many universities actively supporting student-led venture creation. Nonetheless, they also reveal notable

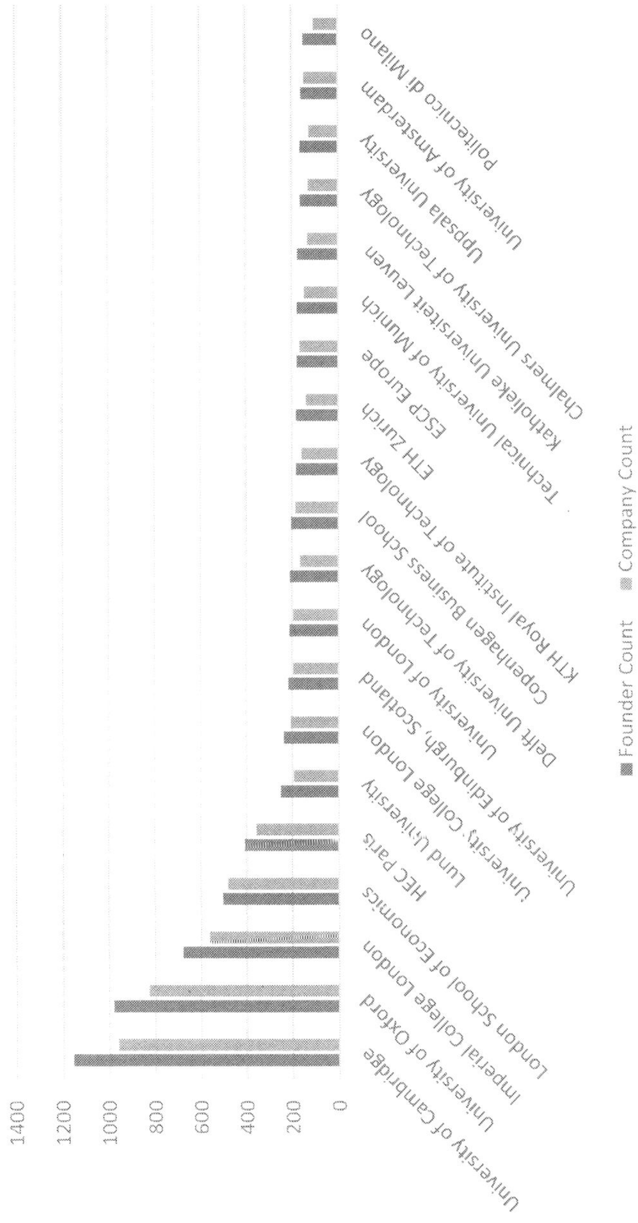

Figure 3.1 Top 20 universities ranked by number of start-ups founded by graduate students in 2022.

Source: Pitchbook University ranking.

geographical differences, requiring an analysis of how entrepreneurship education is structured, where it is most prominent, and what kind of support networks are in place.

A research led in 2023 within the ENTREPRENEDU project (Entreprenedu, 2023) mapped 170 entrepreneurship programs, offered by 136 universities and business schools in 21 countries across Europe. Nearly half (47.6%) of these programs were designed as 2-year Master's programs, while about one-fifth (20%) are undergraduate degrees lasting 3–4 years. Additionally, entrepreneurial education was offered within postgraduate programs such as MBA or executive education.

Geographically, while the number of programs per country varied, a substantial portion—around one-third—appeared concentrated in capital cities. The remaining programs were generally located in dynamic urban areas with active start-up communities, suggesting that universities may serve as bridges between academic knowledge and the business world. A key element arising from the analysis was the strong connection to specific industries or specific areas, sometimes linked to local expertise and the tie to local partners or networks. Indeed, almost 70% of the programs were field-related (e.g. pharma, energy, finance, manufacturing, tourism, and sustainability) and about two-thirds of the programs maintained active connections, including the opportunity to engage in corporate internships and to benefit of expert mentoring, with various actors from the entrepreneurial ecosystem such as business angel communities, corporate partners, research centers, alumni networks, and start-up incubators, among others. Corporate partnerships also took the form of seminars and practical activities throughout the programs (e.g. consultancy programs).

The 2023 mapping offered depicts the integration of acceleration and incubation programs into formal university education. Nonetheless, it also highlights the opportunity to further strengthen the link between academic programs and real-world start-up acceleration, enhancing the practical dimension of entrepreneurship education.

The following paragraph highlights a benchmark of relevant programs that may further shed light on insights from European experiences.

3.3 Entrepreneurship course in European universities: a benchmark analysis

To better understand the structure and content of these programs and to develop a framework for guiding student entrepreneurship initiatives at the university level, 10 different programs offered by the European universities surveyed were further analyzed. They are listed in Table 3.2. The selection of courses was based on the recurrence of specific elements considered relevant in the existing literature on entrepreneurship education. Specifically, certain aspects in program structure were taken into consideration, for their relevance within the existing literature on the effectiveness of entrepreneurship education, namely:

- The presence of a high volume of declared start-up creation
- The existence of extensive connections with the business world (corporations, start-ups, and business angels)
- The presence of an incubator or accelerator within the university

The courses analyzed showed similar formal characteristics. Most of the courses were full-time with classes that take place in person.

Table 3.2 List of university courses selected for benchmark analysis

Course	*University*	*Country*
MSc Innovation, Strategy and Entrepreneurship	Grenoble Ecole de Management	France
Master in Innovation and Entrepreneurship	ESMT Berlin	Germany
Strategic Entrepreneurship and Innovation	King's College London	UK
MSc in Business Administration and Bio-entrepreneurship	Copenhagen Business School	Denmark
Strategic Entrepreneurship	Jönköping University	Sweden
MSc in Innovation and Entrepreneurship	Esade	Spain
MSc in Global Innovation and Entrepreneurship	EmLyon	France
Master in Entrepreneurship	Luiss Business School	Italy
Entrepreneurship and Innovation	SKEMA Business School	France

Source: Authors' own elaboration on online data.

They included a final Master's thesis and an internship which varied in terms of type of partner, duration, and international nature. In terms of content, all courses were based on modular formats that include core technical courses and specific entrepreneurship-related courses. In addition, courses had an interdisciplinary format, where the technical competences (with different topics) come with soft skills that run through all core technical topics.

3.3.1 Core skills

All courses provided by selected universities were characterized by a balance of theory and practice and feature a learning-by-doing approach to entrepreneurship. In terms of the subjects taught, all the analyzed programs included lectures on core topics that cover specific technical competences pertaining to management (e.g. strategy, operations, marketing, sustainability management, and international business), law and finance (e.g. the international corporate legal environment), and innovation (e.g. the future of technology, innovation and business transformation, and platform strategy).

In the field of entrepreneurship, core competences covered venture building, the management of startups, finance for start-ups, international growth, technological start-ups, and scalability.

Furthermore, the courses included specific materials pertaining to skills that are lateral to business, that are summarized in Table 3.3. These courses are designed to inspire personal initiative in the field of entrepreneurship, including interpersonal skills (e.g. negotiation, public speaking, and building a professional network), critical analysis (e.g. challenge labs and research methods), and creativity (e.g. design thinking).

Soft skills are also cultivated through the lab learning model showed in Table 3.4. Labs are meant to enhance participants' soft skills for personal development, equipping them with the tools needed to cultivate an entrepreneurial mindset. Workshops focused on problem-solving skills and learning to adapt to different situations, while refining students' intercultural sensibilities. The workshop model is an integral part of the Master's in Entrepreneurship provided by Luiss Business School. It includes an employability lab, a communications lab, a design thinking lab, a project management lab, a negotiation and analytical thinking lab, and an empathy lab. Labs may also include activities aimed at enhancing digital skills (coding and digital transformation).

Table 3.3 Sample of soft skills included in core courses

Skema	*Newton Lecture Series*
Skema	Challenge lab.—rapid prototyping
Emlyon	Prototyping with Fab
Skema	Design thinking and innovations in user experience
Emlyon	International negotiations
ESMT BERLI	Key writing skills
Grenoble	Languages
Kings college	Research methods
Esade	Creative thinking
ESMT BERLI	Building professional networks
ESMT BERLI	Business presentations
ESMT BERLI	Challenge basics/design thinking
Emlyon	Entrepreneurship and design thinking
ESMT BERLI	Public speaking; conflict in teams
ESMT BERLI	Time management

Source: Our representation of the data collected.

Table 3.4 Competences covered in Luiss Business School's labs

Skill to be developed	*Name*
Empathy	Creativity lab
Empathy	Sustainability
Adaptability	Complex problem solving
Negotiation	Negotiation and conflict management
Analytical thinking	Digital transformation
Resource management	People management
Time management	Project management
Strategic thinking	Design thinking
Communication	How-to-present lab
Employability	Employability lab

Source: Our representation of the data collected.

3.3.2 Field practice

All courses incorporate a strong practical focus alongside traditional learning activities. Actually, the local entrepreneurial network is leveraged by fostering the sharing of ideas and experiences through cross-pollination between academia and business. The practical dimension consists not only of group work and planning but also of individual projects carried out in partnership with companies and start-ups. The range of courses analyzed in this area includes bootcamps, creative workshops, group projects, and summer entrepreneurships. For instance, the Master in Innovation and Entrepreneurship at EST Berlin offers an opportunity during the summer months to take part in practical experience, through an internship at a start-up or by working on an innovation project (Corporate Innovation Project), or to develop one's own company idea with the support of the university incubator (Sustainable Ideation Bootcamp). On the other hand, the ESADE course offers I2P projects in partnership with companies for the resolution of a real business problem. In the summer months, SKEMA offers a comprehensive program that offers a period of immersive study in the entrepreneurial ecosystem of the San Francisco Bay Area and Silicon Valley. The program combines in-depth learning of leading technologies with engineering studies, supplemented by training in innovation management. This approach is designed to foster the development of an effective entrepreneurial mindset and skill set. Group discussions and seminars, which are part of the curriculum, provide support to students.

The courses have a strong international focus and promote student exchange by giving participants the opportunity to spend time abroad with a partner company to develop business projects or work on a consultancy project. In practice, international mobility happens via study abroad or taking part in an exchange with a foreign partner university or international innovation program with a company or start-up in order to develop an entrepreneurial project.

3.3.3 From idea to start-up

All programs had dedicated business incubation or acceleration facilities, supported both by academic incubators (such as the Emlyon Business School Incubator or LUISS Enlabs) and by the broader entrepreneurial ecosystem of the university's location (e.g. Rambla of Innovation for ESADE or Jönköping's Science Park, LV Venture Group for Luiss Business School). The support that universities give to students in creating ventures is reinforced by international cooperation. For example, SKEMA benefits from the support of The Sutardja Center for Entrepreneurship & Technology (SCET), founded by UC Berkeley, which provides support to budding student entrepreneurs.

The courses offer students the opportunity to be assigned a business mentor to support their entrepreneurial ideas. In the model implemented by Copenhagen Business School, the mentor is directly assigned by the company hosting the internship. Meanwhile, at Luiss Business School, industry professionals guide participants through a deal process during the program.

3.4 Toward a European student entrepreneurship model

The systematization of benchmarks about the characteristics of the selected course at the European level allowed for the development of an initial framework for successful university entrepreneurship education, which is shown in Figure 3.2.

In the figure, it is possible to identify several key areas:

- Technical and entrepreneurial skills
- Soft skills
- Active practice
- International exposure
- Active support for venture creation

Each area is characterized by specific elements that contribute to the success of the courses.

Furthermore, when considering the structure of entrepreneurship courses at the European level, and comparing them with the EntreComp model developed by the European Union and presented in Chapter 2, university courses seem to predominantly focus on strengthening key competencies related to "into action" and "ideas and opportunities," emphasizing practical application and entrepreneurial thinking. These competencies are hybridized to offer a holistic view of entrepreneurship that inspires entrepreneurial thinking by leveraging activity development with cross-pollination between the academic and business worlds and active exchange as a driver to develop creativity and new, immediately actionable business ideas.

As compared to EntreComp, here relevant aspects include the value assigned to digital technology management competencies and international mobility as factors to stimulate openness to new ideas. The courses value centrality for students to build their own networks with the business community during the courses, through peer exchange and continuous feedback linked to mentoring activities. Literature

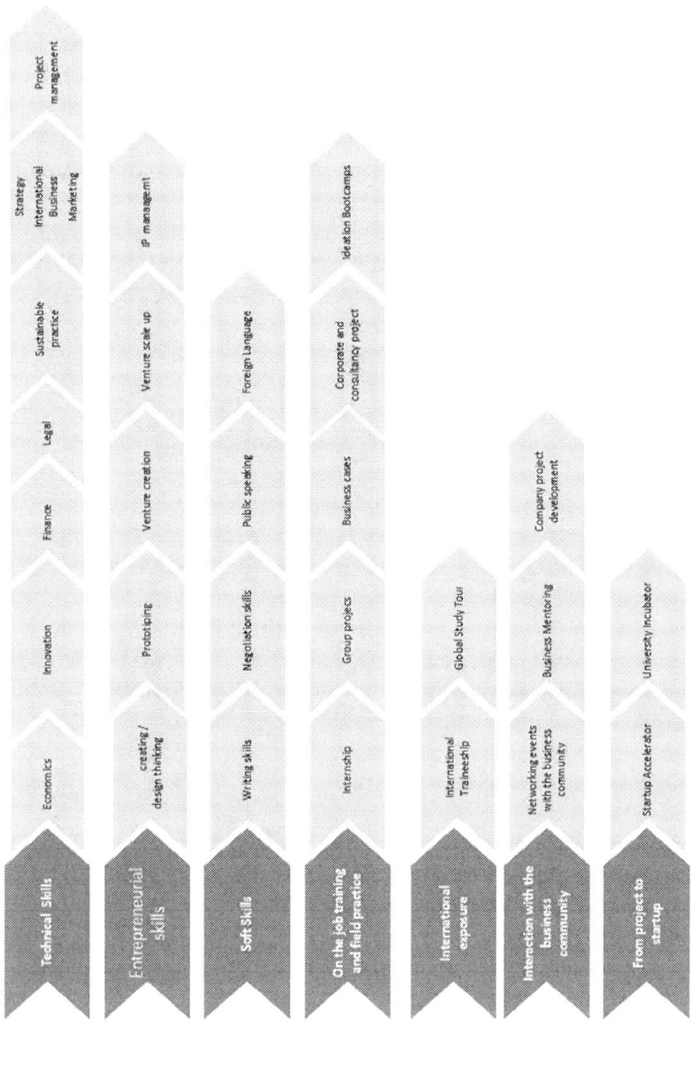

Figure 3.2 Framework of European student entrepreneurship.

recognizes networks as drivers of success for student entrepreneurship, capable of having an impact on the motivation of participants along with self-efficacy in the courses (Politis et al., 2012). European entrepreneurship courses integrate this concept throughout the learning experience, actively leveraging partnerships with the business ecosystem to provide students with hands-on interaction and exchange opportunities. The systematization of the success factors of the University Programs European level is presented in Figure 3.2.

3.5 Conclusions

Although entrepreneurship education developed later in Europe than in the United States, European universities have managed to establish themselves as catalysts in their regions for the creation of new student-led entrepreneurial initiatives. This phenomenon is characterized by universities creating infrastructure for technology transfer, supporting students in developing new business initiatives, and linking them to the business community. Data collected from mapping entrepreneurship courses at the regional level shows that student entrepreneurship is highly concentrated in advanced entrepreneurial ecosystems where students tend to develop their ventures in integrated support structures within their academic institutions. Indeed, academic institutions that have successful programs demonstrate the capacity to foster innovative entrepreneurial activities.

The benchmark analysis further highlighted that if university courses are to be drivers for creating new ventures, a mix of factors must be present, including:

- Integration of theoretical knowledge with practical and experiential activities
- Development of soft skills in the areas of creativity, critical thinking, and relationship and communication abilities
- External exposure, which becomes a key element and is achieved through:
- International mobility
- Involvement in on-the-job internships at start-ups, established companies, and consulting firms

The framework shows that the design of entrepreneurship courses should follow multidisciplinary approaches that aim to creating an entrepreneurial mindset, developing soft skills, and focusing on relationship building and analytical skills and foster creativity.

The courses should support the development of ideas and training through "learning by doing" methodologies and interaction with the entrepreneurial ecosystem, following the logic of "integrated educational programs." Collaboration with foreign universities and companies is key in the European model, and it is seen as a way to allow students to develop an international viewpoint and learn from experiences across borders.

Notes

1 Officially launched in 1999 within the framework of the Bologna Declaration (adopted at the Conference of Ministers of Education on June 19, 1999).

2 The conference was held in Tirana on May 2024. The official communiqué is available at: https://ehea.info/page-ehea-ministerial-conference-2024

3 The Index is released by Redstone in collaboration with the Munich-based think tank AlpMomentum and the Brussels-based European Startup Network (ESN). The index is based on the analysis of 457 entrepreneurially active European universities and 7,555 start-ups originating from these universities.

4 The 2023 PitchBook University ranking is based on the total number of founders whose companies received a first round of venture funding between Jan. 1, 2013 and Sept. 1, 2023. The analysis is based on PitchBook data for global VC investment as well as the educational information of more than 150,000 founders.

5 The Redstone University Startup Index 2024, June 2024. Available at: www.redstone.vc/research/redstone-university-startup-index

References

Bergmann, H., Hundt, C. and Sternberg, R. (2014). "What makes student entrepreneurs? – On the relevance (and irrelevance) of the university and the regional context for student start-ups Heiko Bergmann Christian Hundt," *Small Business Economics*, Vol. 47, No 1 pp. 1–36.

Chaudhary, R. (2017). "Demographic factors, personality and entrepreneurial inclination," *Education + Training*, Vol. 59 No. 2, pp. 171–187.

Entreprenedu (2023). Inventory of success cases and go-to business scenarios: https://entreprenedu.eu/wp-content/uploads/2024/11/WP2_Inventory-of-the-success-cases-and-go-to-business-scenario.pdf

Forliano, C., De Bernardi, P. and Yahiaoui, D. (2021). "Entrepreneurial universities: A bibliometric analysis within the business and management domains," *Technological Forecasting and Social Change*, Vol. 165, pp. 1–16. https://doi.org/10.1016/j.techfore.2020.120522

Kushnir, I. (2016). "The role of the Bologna process in defining Europe," *European Educational Research Journal*, Vol. 15, No. 6, pp. 664–675.

López-Núñez, M.I., Rubio-Valdehita, S., Díaz-Ramiro, E. and Martín-Seoane, G. (2021). "The entrepreneurial profile of university students: A predictive model," *Revista de Educacion*, Vol. 2021, No. 392, pp. 11–32.

Maheshwari, G., Kha, K.L. and Arokiasamy, A.R.A. (2022). "Factors affecting students' entrepreneurial intentions: A systematic review (2005–2022) for future directions in theory and practice," *Management Review Quarterly*, Vol. 73, pp. 1905–1970. https://doi.org/10.1007/s11301-022-00289-2

Politis, D., Winborg, J. and Dahlstrand, Å.L. (2012). "Exploring the resource logic of student entrepreneurs," *International Small Business Journal*, Vol. 30, No. 6, pp. 659–683.

Sá, E.S. and Pinho, J.C.M.R. (2019). "Effect of entrepreneurial framework conditions on R&D transfer to new and growing firms: The case of European Union innovation-driven countries," *Technological Forecasting and Social Change*, Vol. 141, No. December 2018, pp. 47–58.

Wilson, K. (2008). "Chapter 5: Entrepreneurship Education in Europe." OECD, 2008, Available at SSRN: https://ssrn.com/abstract=1392369

Entrepreneurship and Higher Education.

4 Collaborative strategies for student entrepreneurship

From mentoring to venture building

Contributors: Abel Fernandez, Jacopo Piccagli from EBAN, Paola Belingheri, Christian Lechner from LUIS, Katrin Singer-Coudoux, Henry Nicolai Buxmann from Fraunhofer IPK

4.1 Addressing regional innovation disparities in the EU

Entrepreneurs in regions with emerging or moderate innovation levels often face distinctive barriers, such as restricted access to resources, inadequate support networks, and a less established entrepreneurial culture (European Union 2023).

Investing in entrepreneurial education in less innovative regions can transform local economies by fostering self-reliance and promoting homegrown innovation. Access to high-quality programs equips students and aspiring entrepreneurs with the skills and confidence to start businesses, generating local employment and diversifying economic activities. This reduces dependence on external markets and builds resilience against economic shocks.

These strategies are essential in order to bridge uneven distribution of entrepreneurial education and resources across Europe; actually, there are significant innovation gaps among European regions (Xie 2024). In fact, while some areas benefit from thriving ecosystems with access to cutting-edge education, mentorship, and funding, others struggle to provide even the foundational tools for entrepreneurial success. These differences can be seen on the European Innovation Scoreboard where innovation performance among regions varies.[1] Countries classified as "innovation leaders," such as Germany, Sweden, and Finland, are home to well-developed ecosystems that offer comprehensive entrepreneurial education and access to funding. These regions also boast strong networks connecting universities, businesses, and government entities, creating fertile ground for entrepreneurship to flourish. In contrast, "modest" and "moderate" innovators, such as Bulgaria,

DOI: 10.4324/9781003607649-5

Greece, and Italy, have weaknesses in terms of attractiveness of their research systems and in terms of the level of investments in R&D. This is tied with a lack of guidance for student entrepreneurs to navigate the complexities of building and scaling a business.

Funding opportunities are another major hurdle. Entrepreneurs in less innovative regions frequently encounter challenges in securing capital because investors tend to be concentrated in established innovation regions. This creates a vicious cycle: without sufficient resources, start-ups struggle to grow, discouraging further investment and limiting the development of local entrepreneurial ecosystems. As a result, talented individuals in underdeveloped regions are often forced to seek opportunities elsewhere, contributing to a "brain drain" that further weakens these areas (Kaufmann and Miki, 2015).

Addressing these disparities is essential not only for regional development but also for fostering a more cohesive and resilient European innovation landscape. Creating equal opportunities in entrepreneurial education and resources is a critical step in addressing regional disparities. Efforts to bridge this divide by promoting inclusive entrepreneurship opportunities can unlock significant benefits, fostering the creation of an environment that improves resilience and innovation across all regions of Europe (Henry et al., 2024).

Research by Autio et al. (2014) highlights the critical role that regional innovation ecosystems play in the success of entrepreneurial ventures. Furthermore, literature suggests that mentoring is most effective when adapted to the specific needs and contexts of individuals (Mouammer and Bazan 2021). Promoting cross-border collaboration and leveraging the strengths of different regions help create shared knowledge and the creation of entrepreneurial ecosystems providing the spread of value creation at regional level, innovation leaders with fresh perspectives and opportunities to address untapped markets and create new ventures (Stam and van de Ven, 2021).

Further, strengthening regional entrepreneurial ecosystems can create the conditions for enhancing innovation spillover and creating a supportive environment for start-ups, which can contribute to enhancing the competitiveness of the European Union internal market (Content et al., 2020).

The role of academia is paramount for the creation of effective entrepreneurial ecosystems across European regions. By implementing new pedagogical approaches rooted in experiential learning, academia can offer targeted programs that expose students to practical entrepreneurial challenges while fostering collaboration between academia and industry. This cross-pollination creates an environment where innovative ideas can be tested, refined, and transformed into viable ventures. Ultimately, such initiatives contribute to a more equitable distribution of resources and opportunities (Mazzarol et al., 2016).

In addition to the mobility, professional development, and interuniversity exchange activities established at the European level as part of Erasmus +, mentorship and venture-building programs in universities are also important in fostering entrepreneurial ecosystems. This is demonstrated by the experience of the ENTREPRENEDU[2] project, which has developed a comprehensive set of programs to address gaps in entrepreneurship education. In the next section, we will explore how ENTREPRENEDU integrates mentorship and skills development into a venture-building program to equip students with the tools they need to create and grow impactful ventures, accelerate the growth of start-ups, and build a foundation for the sustainable success of student-led ventures.

4.2 The role of mentoring for innovative practice in regions with a lower concentration of start-ups

Academic research has acknowledged the relevance of mentoring to bridge disparities across regions. Effective mentoring programs can help spread innovative practices to mid-tier and less innovative regions by fostering strategic goal-setting, leveraging local networks, adapting to feedback, prioritizing inclusive business models, and equipping entrepreneurs with practical skills and a proactive mindset. Specifically, tailored mentorship programs that are customized to the needs of a particular institutional setting—integrating local and global insights—can empower entrepreneurs in less innovative or resource-constrained environments to achieve sustainable growth and innovation.

Lingelbach et al. (2005) observed that entrepreneurs in less innovative areas who capitalize on informal networks and local community assets tend to secure the resources and support necessary for business expansion (Lingelbach, 2005). Similarly, Miller and Wedell-Wedellsborg (2013) identified that entrepreneurs who continuously assess and adjust their products or services based on feedback are more likely to achieve product-market fit, which is crucial in resource-limited settings (Miller and Wendell-Wedellsborg, 2013). Moreover, Naudé (2013) stressed that entrepreneurship training programs tailored to the practical and contextual needs of entrepreneurs in emerging regions tend to be more impactful in addressing the specific challenges within these areas (Naudé 2013).

4.3 Designing mentoring programs to foster entrepreneurship

Mentoring has to do with a reciprocal relationship that is established between a mentor and a mentee with the goal of providing support, counseling, and role modelling that benefits participants in terms of direction and support for career development (Eby & Robertson, 2021).

4.3.1 The role of mentoring to support entrepreneurship

Mentoring plays a crucial role in terms of the competency development of entrepreneurs for the creation and success of new start-ups, as it guides founders through the complexities of building a business from the ground up (Rechter and Avnimelech, 2024). In fact, in a fast-paced, innovation-driven world, mentors provide not only knowledge and experience but also socio-emotional support, helping new entrepreneurs navigate challenges and avoid common pitfalls (Nabi et al., 2021). Mentoring for entrepreneurs provides a structured framework in which novice entrepreneurs, or mentees, receive guidance from seasoned business practitioners.

Assenova (2020) showed that mentoring for early-stage entrepreneurs led to an increase in revenue, profit, and employment growth for underprivileged entrepreneurs. Furthermore, mentoring influences the culture within start-ups, promoting adherence to foundational principles and cultivating an environment conducive to constructive problem-solving (Brodie et al. 2017).

Mentors often offer their services in specific programs that are pivotal in developing vital entrepreneurial skills and advancing business growth. Furthermore, research by Cope and Watts (2000) underscored the significance of these tailored programs in offering support that is critically aligned with the mentees' specific business development stages. Such individualized support not only addresses the immediate needs of entrepreneurs but also profoundly impacts their self-efficacy, enhancing their belief in their capabilities to succeed (St-Jean et al. 2018).

4.3.2 From online mentoring to hybrid mentoring

The recent literature has begun to focus on mentorship in digital settings, highlighting its benefits, particularly the strengthening of the relationship between mentor and mentee and the increase in opportunities for interaction. Following the development of online mentoring, Kakouris (2017) introduced a transformative pedagogical approach in Greek entrepreneurship education through the TeleCC online platform (Kakouris, 2017). This constructivist model emphasizes cognitive development through interactive and reflective learning experiences. By fostering critical thinking and meta-learning, it represents a substantial shift from traditional mentoring to a dynamic, participant-driven educational practice, potentially enriching lifelong and inclusive learning in entrepreneurship. Kakouris (2009) further emphasizes the importance of specialized online platforms to support experiential entrepreneurial learning effectively in European higher education. These platforms are crucial for facilitating action learning and supporting working groups beyond traditional classroom settings (Kakouris, 2009).

Despite the relevant benefits of mentoring in digital settings, the shift towards online mentoring programs introduces new challenges, particularly in establishing the depth of connection that face-to-face interactions facilitate. Online platforms, while providing wide-reaching access, lack the nonverbal communication cues, such as body language and eye contact, that are essential in building trust and rapport between mentors and mentees (Lall et al., 2022). The asynchronous nature of many online interactions also impedes the flow of real-time feedback, which is important for timely guidance and adjustment in the learning process (Hooley et al. 2016; Walsh 2016).

To address these mentoring challenges, a hybrid approach that combines the strengths of both asynchronous and synchronous learning methods can be applied. Asynchronous learning allows mentees the flexibility to engage with the material at their own pace, which can make the mentoring more accessible and inclusive, accommodating various learning styles and personal schedules (Chang et al. 2014). In fact, synchronous learning, through real-time interactions such as video conferences, mimics the immediacy and engagement of traditional classroom settings. This method enhances the engagement and allows for dynamic discussions and immediate feedback, which are vital for an effective learning experience (Mullen 2021). By incorporating both asynchronous and synchronous learning formats into the curriculum, mentees can benefit from a blended approach that combines the advantages of self-paced learning with real-time engagement. This hybrid model can offer a comprehensive learning experience, cater to different learning preferences, and maximize the effectiveness of mentoring programs (Dada et al., 2019).

4.3.3 Building mentoring programs

The structure of mentoring programs is pivotal in creating successful mentorship initiatives. The program should embrace progressive learning, which involves designing a curriculum that gradually transitions from basic to more complex entrepreneurial concepts and practices. This approach allows participants to build on their knowledge base and skills systematically, ensuring a solid foundation of understanding before advancing to more challenging topics (DuBois et al., 2011).

To effectively support mentees through progressive stages of learning, mentoring support should be adaptable and responsive to the changing needs of the participants as they advance through the program. This support includes tailored guidance and feedback that align with the mentees' evolving levels of expertise and challenges (Rigg and O'Dwyer, 2012; Russell, 2007).

Additionally, fostering autonomy and self-efficacy is crucial in these programs. As mentees progress, they should be encouraged to gradually take on more responsibility in decision-making and problem-solving, thus empowering them to take ownership of their learning journey and business development (Sarri 2011; Seet et al. 2018). Incorporating opportunities for reflection and self-assessment at each stage of the program can further aid mentees in consolidating their learning, identifying areas for improvement, and setting realistic goals for future development (Garcia-Molsosa et al. 2021).

Finally, conducting a demand analysis for entrepreneurial mentoring is critical in understanding the specific needs and psychological resources of entrepreneurs, such as self-efficacy and optimism. Such an analysis can guide the development of mentoring programs that effectively address these needs, enhancing entrepreneurial intentions and outcomes (Ayodele et al., 2022; Baluku et al., 2020; Nabi et al., 2021).

4.4 Case study: The ENTREPRENEDU mentoring program

4.4.1 Program objective and delivery

As part of the ENTREPRENEDU[3] project, an online mentoring program was designed with the objective of equipping young entrepreneurs from the emerging and moderately innovative countries of Italy, Greece, and Bulgaria with the necessary skills to create successful start-ups or improve the performance of an already existing start-up (Singer-Coudoux, Buxmann, Will, 2024). A demand analysis was carried out as an initial step in order to examine the needs and experiences of the participants through semistructured interviews led by two Fraunhofer IPK researchers and one research assistant to ensure consistency in data collection and interpretation (Buxmann et al., 2024). Each of these hour-long sessions followed a structured guideline, aiming to identify the unique entrepreneurial needs of the participating teams. A thematic analysis of the interview data uncovered clusters of key needs across the teams, which formed the basis for defining six core mentoring topics. The idea was also to shape the program's curriculum in order to directly address participants' specific needs. The six key areas addressed by the ENTREPRENEDU mentoring program included:

1. Business model development
2. Crafting value propositions
3. Technical feasibility and product development
4. Investment readiness
5. Comprehensive business planning
6. Access to finance

Each demand was transformed into one mentoring module, with one of the project's mentoring partners responsible for each. Then, each module was crafted to support the overall objectives of the program, with clear learning outcomes specified to guide participants on what they could expect to achieve in each module. Additionally, the program's curriculum detailed the sequence in which topics would be introduced, the timeline for the program, and the approach for assessing progress and delivering feedback to participants.

This also helped form the foundation for the modules in the venture-building program. Results for interviews showed that participating teams and start-ups had varying skill levels and experiences.

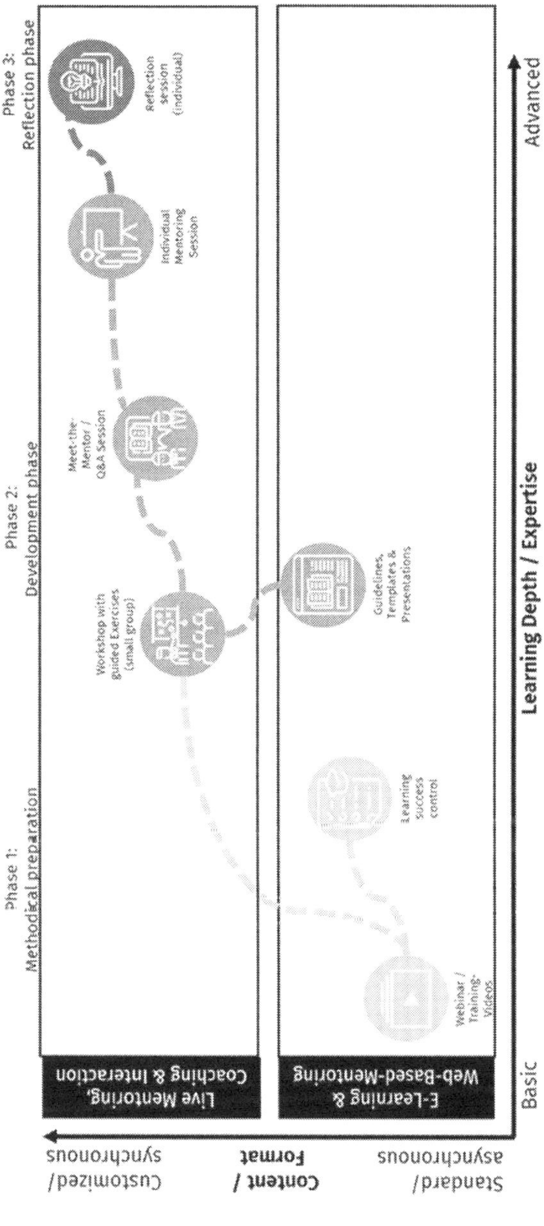

Figure 4.1 ENTREPRENEDU mentorir g program structure.

This was taken into consideration, leading to the adoption of a blended learning approach that combined both asynchronous and synchronous components of increasing complexity. This structure allowed participants to engage with material suited to their skill levels while benefiting from the flexibility of online participation from wherever they were located. Figure 4.1 illustrates the program's three distinct phases, outlining the mentoring units, content structure, and depth of learning.

Phase one focused on foundational knowledge, with standardized content delivery through online formats like webinars and training videos. This introductory content was the same for all participants and included a 1-hour, knowledge-assessment quiz. Each mentoring module contained three training videos, each approximately 1 hour in length, with the complexity of the content increasing progressively through the sequence.

The second phase, centered around skill development, offered more tailored learning experiences aligned with participants' specific needs. Delivered in a live-mentoring format, this phase incorporated workshops, Q&A sessions, and individualized mentoring. Each mentoring partner conducted a 2-hour workshop for cohort participants, utilizing tools like Concept and Miro boards to facilitate peer feedback and interactive learning. After the workshop, a 1-hour Q&A session allowed participants to review and discuss the material, followed by 2 hours of personalized mentoring from each partner to focus on individual needs and circumstances.

The final phase emphasized reflection and feedback, providing a 1-hour session with each mentoring partner. In these sessions, participants evaluated their progress, reviewed achievements, and set future goals with their mentors' guidance.

In total, the mentoring program offered each participant 10 hours of mentorship across all phases, aimed at maximizing team potential and promoting long-term success. With six mentoring organizations involved, each start-up in the first cohort received a combined 60 hours of mentorship support.

4.4.2 Results of the ENTREPRENEDU mentoring program

To assess the mentoring program's impact, feedback was collected through structured interviews. This qualitative approach allowed participants to reflect deeply on their experiences, addressing key areas, such as skill development, business-model refinement, and goal-setting. Moreover, the semi-structured interviewing technique allowed for a detailed and dynamic exchange that highlighted both the program's strengths and areas for improvement. Overall, mentees found the program transformative, noting substantial progress in refining business ideas, setting measurable goals, and building essential entrepreneurial skills. While mentor guidance and the collaborative learning environment were both highly valued, some participants found peer interactions less beneficial due to diverse business backgrounds. Feedback on individual modules was largely positive, particularly for those focused on business models, value propositions, and funding, although participants suggested refining module sequencing and providing additional support in areas like human resources and leadership.

The program's technical aspects were generally well-received, though scheduling challenges and prompted suggestions for a more streamlined process. Across cohorts, participants expressed high satisfaction and recommended further module depth, extended timelines, and more flexible content access to enhance learning. The feedback further highlighted the ENTREPRENEDU mentoring program's positive impact on entrepreneurial development, with participants showing appreciation for its structured guidance and the opportunity to advance their business ideas. Mentees reported growth in strategic planning, goal-setting, and entrepreneurial skills, finding the program to be transformative overall.

The ENTREPRENEDU mentoring program case further demonstrates the transformative potential of mentorship and its pivotal role in fostering entrepreneurial competencies. It also serves as a guide for the implementation of further programs to support student entrepreneurship.

Furthermore, its findings underscored the value of tailored guidance, progressive learning, and hybrid educational models. Leveraging these insights, the venture-building program extended the scope of mentorship to reach a wider audience, ensuring alignment with both regional and individual needs.

4.5 The ENTREPRENEDU venture-building program

4.5.1 From mentoring to venture-building

The findings and success of the ENTREPRENEDU mentoring program directly informed the design of the venture-building program, allowing for a natural progression from guided mentoring to a more comprehensive entrepreneurial education model. In fact, the ENTREPRENEDU mentoring experience served as the basis for the development of a structured, comprehensive framework designed to empower students with the skills, tools, and knowledge necessary to create a sustainable and innovative program for venture building.

Specifically, the mentoring program revealed the importance of aligning educational content with the specific needs of aspiring entrepreneurs. This was achieved through a detailed demand analysis, which identified the unique challenges faced by participants in each region. These findings directly influenced the design of the venture-building program, ensuring that each module was tailored to address real-world entrepreneurial challenges.

Following the phases of the mentoring program, the venture-building program adopted a three-phase approach:

- **Foundational knowledge:** Standardized learning materials introduced participants to key entrepreneurial concepts.
- **Skill development:** Interactive workshops and individualized mentoring helped participants apply their knowledge to practical scenarios.
- **Reflective growth:** Mentorship focused on evaluating progress, refining strategies, and setting future goals.

This three-pronged framework ensured that participants progressed systematically, building their capabilities while receiving continuous support.

The hybrid approach of the mentoring program was applied to the venture-building program to accommodate a larger, more diverse audience. Hence the venture-building program envisaged:

- **Asynchronous learning:** Participants accessed webinars, quizzes, and other digital resources to engage with the content at their own pace.
- **Synchronous Engagement:** Real-time workshops, Q&A sessions, and personalized mentoring sessions provided opportunities for deeper interaction and immediate feedback.

Moreover, one of the most important peculiarities of the venture-building program was its transition from a focused mentoring initiative to a scalable educational framework.

4.6 The ENTREPRENEDU venture-building program

The **ENTREPRENEDU venture-building program** serves as a cornerstone of entrepreneurial education, offering a structured, multi-phase approach to nurturing the entrepreneurial potential of students across Europe. This section outlines the program's key components, focusing on its modular structure, blended learning approach, and integration of practical tools and mentorship. Developed collaboratively under the scheme of the ENTREPRENEDU project and led by the European Business Angel Network (EBAN), involving LUISS University, the University of Thessaly, and CleanTech Bulgaria as academic partners, the program aimed to bridge the gap between academic theory and the practical demands of entrepreneurship, equipping students with essential knowledge, skills, and experiences to succeed in the innovation-driven global economy. Table 4.1. shows the structure of the venture-building program designed by ENTREPRENEDU"

The program was designed to:

1 **Provide comprehensive learning:** Equip students with the tools and methodologies to navigate the entrepreneurial journey, from ideation to scaling a business.
2 **Foster practical application:** Emphasize real-world problem-solving through case studies, mentoring, and project-based learning.
3 **Encourage regional adaptation:** Tailor content to reflect the diverse innovation capacities of participating countries, ensuring inclusivity and relevance.
4 **Support sustainability and growth:** Incorporate modules that align with the sustainable development goals (SDGs) and encourage green business practices.

The venture-building program envisaged the creation of a "venture-building syllabus." The syllabus is a comprehensive educational framework that outlines the tasks that universities and educators can follow in order to equip students with the skills and knowledge necessary to successfully navigate the entrepreneurial journey. The venture-building syllabus is a practical guide that aims to provide students with a pathway not only to increase their resilience in the face of the challenges associated with starting a business but also to enhance their ability to create scalable and sustainable ventures in the long term. The structure of the curriculum is comprehensive and adaptable, yet

Table 4.1 Structure of the venture-building program

Module 2: Solution Development and Validation, Crafting Value Proposition

- **Objective:** Enable students to design and validate solutions that effectively address identified problems.
  - **Content:** Frameworks such as the **Value Proposition Canvas** to ensure product-market fit.
  - Techniques for prototyping, A/B testing, and pilot studies.
  - Incorporation of design thinking to iterate on solutions.
- **Activities:**
  - Practical exercises in crafting compelling value propositions.
  - Collaborative prototyping workshops to refine solutions.
  - Real-world case studies of start-ups that successfully validated their ideas.

Module 3: Market Discovery

- **Objective:** Equip students with skills to conduct market research, understand customer segmentation, and identify growth opportunities.
- **Content:**
  - Fundamentals of market research and tools like SWOT analysis.
  - Techniques for leveraging digital tools for data collection and analysis.
  - Strategies for identifying and targeting niche markets.
- **Activities:**
  - Hands-on market research projects, including competitor analysis and customer profiling.
  - Role-playing exercises to simulate customer interactions.
  - Use of tools like the **Market Opportunity Navigator** to assess viability.

Module 4: Business Model Development

- **Objective:** Help students build scalable and sustainable business models.
- **Content:**
  - Use of the **Business Model Canvas** to map out business components.
  - Exploration of revenue streams, value delivery mechanisms, and customer engagement strategies.
  - Emphasis on sustainable business practices and aligning with ESG (Environmental, Social, and Governance) criteria.
- **Activities:**
  - Group projects to design business models for hypothetical or real ventures.
  - Analysis of case studies demonstrating innovative business models.
  - Interactive sessions on the importance of adaptability and resilience in business planning.

Table 4.1 (Continued)

Module 5: Access to Finance and Funding

• **Objective:** Prepare students to secure funding through effective pitching and financial planning.
• **Content:**
  • Overview of funding sources, including venture capital, angel investment, and crowdfunding.
  • Techniques for crafting compelling investment pitches.
  • Financial planning, including revenue forecasting and cash flow management.
• **Activities:**
  • Pitch simulation exercises, with feedback from mentors and peers.
  • Workshops on financial statement preparation.
  • Guest speaker sessions featuring investors sharing insights on successful funding strategies.

Source: Based on work of the authors.

capable of meeting the diverse needs of students in different academic settings to secure funding and scale a business.

The curriculum included in the syllabus is structured to guide students through the entrepreneurial journey in a logical and practical way, providing them with the tools they need to succeed in real-life scenarios. In addition, the curriculum is a dynamic tool for universities to create their own venture-building programs consistent with regional characteristics, leveraging local case studies, industry connections, and educational traditions.

The venture-building syllabus has already been experimented by three partner institutions as part of the ENTREPRENEDU projects. These educational institutions included LUISS (Italy), University of Thessaly (Greece), and CleanTech Bulgaria (Bulgaria). The participating universities integrated the syllabus of the venture-building program into their university curriculum. More specifically, these experiments were implemented in the context of the early stages of the start-up process, considering that most students have little or no previous experience with the topic.

Further experiments of the syllabus that were held by CleanTech Bulgaria (CTBG) saw the adaptation of the syllabus to a vocational training setting. Hence, a focus that placed more emphasis on practical emphasis training was adopted by putting the emphasis on hands-on exercises, real-world simulations, and project-based learning through

Figure 4.2 QR Code for accessing the venture-building syllabus.

each module, by breaking down the larger modules into smaller, and easily affordable units, to make the course more engaging and accessible. Vocational program students benefited from shorter, modular units that allowed them for immediate implementation of the knowledge acquired during the venture-building program.

These experimentations allowed for three key features of the academic model to be identified. In particular, the importance of **localized content:** Modules were adapted to reflect the unique entrepreneurial ecosystems of each region, addressing specific barriers such as funding gaps and limited networks.

Another feature was **collaborative learning:** Students engaged in peer-to-peer feedback activities, fostering a collaborative environment that enriched their learning experience; and lastly **sustainability and growth:** The program emphasized sustainable business practices, preparing participants to align their ventures with broader societal and environmental goals.

4.7 Conclusions

Mentoring and incubator programs emerge as fundamental infrastructure for entrepreneurial development, providing students with structured pathways to transform theoretical understanding into tangible business opportunities. These platforms do more than transfer knowledge; they create transformative experiences that shape entrepreneurial mindsets, build confidence, and provide critical networks that can support student entrepreneurs throughout their venture-building journey. It also demonstrates the effectiveness of structured and collaborative approaches in addressing the uneven distribution of entrepreneurial education and resources. By targeting underserved regions, fostering inclusive ecosystems, and emphasizing cross-border collaboration, such initiatives highlight the potential to unlock untapped talent and drive regional development. These efforts not only prepare individuals to thrive as entrepreneurs but also catalyze economic and social progress in areas traditionally left behind.

The ENTREPRENDU experience showed the importance of adopting tailored approaches to venture-building programs and mentoring that should be able to adapt to the contexts of the higher education institutions in which they are implemented in order to better address regional disparities in entrepreneurial education through customized content and practical support. The cases also show the relevance of **feedback mechanisms,** such as surveys and evaluations in refining the program, ensuring its ongoing relevance and effectiveness.

Finally, the ENTREPRENEDU experience acknowledges the relevance of **integrating digital tools in mentoring and venture-building programs** not only to broaden their accessibility, especially for entrepreneurs in remote or underserved areas but also to consider in the course structure themes related to sustainability and social entrepreneurship to prepare young entrepreneurs to address contemporary and future challenges, in line with global trends in innovation and responsible business practices.

Notes

1 European Commission. https://research-and-innovation.ec.europa.eu/statistics/performance-indicators/european-innovation-scoreboard_en

2 ENTREPRENEDU is an initiative funded by the European Innovation Council and the SMEs Executive Agency (EISMEA) with an aim of enhancing entrepreneurial ecosystems for education. The ENTREPRENEDU consortium brings together different innovation stakeholders and educational entities from six different European countries—Italy, Bulgaria, Greece, Belgium, Germany, and Ireland. The ENTREPRENEDU initiative will support the 12 most viable and promising ideas and concepts from the early stages to the commercialization of their solutions. In this

way, ENTREPRENEDU will enable a highly replicable model to provide business know-how for young Europeans to be deployed in European universities.

3 ENTREPRENEDU is an initiative funded by the European Innovation Council and the SMEs Executive Agency (EISMEA) with the aim of enhancing entrepreneurial ecosystems for education. The ENTREPRENEDU consortium brings together different innovation stakeholders and educational entities from six different European countries—Italy, Bulgaria, Greece, Belgium, Germany, and Ireland. The ENTREPRENEDU initiative supports the 12 most viable and promising ideas and concepts from the early stages to the commercialization of their solutions. In that way, ENTREPRENEDU enables a highly replicable model to provide business know-how for young Europeans to be deployed in European Universities.

References

Assenova, V.A. (2020). "Early-stage venture incubation and mentoring promote learning, scaling, and profitability among disadvantaged entrepreneurs", *Organization Science*, Vol. 31, No. 6, pp. 1560–1578. doi:10.1287/orsc.2020.1367

Autio, E., Kenney, M., Mustar, P., Siegel, D. and Wright, M. (2014). "Entrepreneurial innovation: The importance of context", *Research Policy*, Vol. 43, No. (7), pp. 1097–1108. doi:10.1016/j.respol.2014.01.015

Ayodele, T.O., Ekemode, B.G., and Kajimo-Shakantu, K. (2022). "Bridging the gap in real estate enterprise: The impact of mentoring on entrepreneurial intentions of real estate students in Nigeria", *Property Management*, Vol. 40, No. 4, pp. 484–509. doi:10.1108/pm-02-2021-0015

Baluku, M.M., Matagi, L. and Otto, K. (2020). "Exploring the link between mentoring and intangible outcomes of entrepreneurship: The mediating role of self-efficacy and moderating effects of gender", *Frontiers in Psychology*, Vol. 11, pp. 1556. doi:10.3389/fpsyg.2020.01556

Brodie, J., van Saane, S.H. and Osowska, R. (2017). "Help wanted". In: *Industry and Higher Education*, Vol. 31, No. 2, pp. 122–131. doi:10.1177/0950422217691666

Buxmann, H., Singer-Coudoux, K. and Houssni, K. (2024). "Tailoring entrepreneurial education: Demand-driven insights for an entrepreneurial online mentoring program", *European Conference on e-Learning*, Vol. 23, pp. 52–59. doi:10.34190/ecel.23.1.2852

Chang, T.P., Pham, P.K., Sobolewski, B., Doughty, C.B., Jamal N., Kwan, K.Y. et al. (2014). "Pediatric emergency medicine asynchronous e-learning: A multicenter randomized controlled Solomon four-group study," *Academic Emergency Medicine*, Vol. 21, No. 8, pp. 912–919. doi:10.1111/acem.12434

Content, J., Bosma, N., Jordaan, J., and Sanders, M. (2020). "Entrepreneurial ecosystems, entrepreneurial activity and economic growth: New evidence from European regions", *Regional Studies*, Vol. 54, No. (8), pp. 1007–1019. doi:10.1080/00343404.2019.1680827

Cope, J. and Watts, G. (2000). Learning by doing – An exploration of experience, critical incidents and reflection in entrepreneurial learning", *International Journal of Entrepreneurial Behavior & Research*, Vol. 6, No. (3), pp. 104–124. doi:10.1108/13552550010346208

Dada, G.E., Alkali, H.A. and Oyewola, D. (2019). "An investigation into the effectiveness of asynchronous and synchronous E-learning mode on students' academic performance in National Open University (NOUN), Maiduguri Centre", *IJMECS*, Vol. 11, No. 5, pp. 54–64. doi:10.5815/ijmecs.2019.05.06

DuBois, D.L., Portillo, N., Rhodes, J.E., Silverthorn, N. and Valentine, J.C. (2011). "How effective are mentoring programs for youth? A systematic assessment of the evidence", *Psychological Science in the Public Interest*, Vol. 12, No. (2), pp. 57–91. doi:10.1177/1529100611414806

Eby, L.T. and Robertson, M.M. (2020). "The psychology of workplace mentoring relationships", *Annual Review of Organizational Psychology and Organizational Behavior*, Vol. 7, No. 1, pp. 75–100. Available at: https://ssrn.com/abstract=3550371

European Union (Hg.) (2023): European Innovation Scoreboard 2023. Online verfügbar unter https://research-and-innovation.ec.europa.eu/statistics/performance-indicators/european-innovation-scoreboard_en#documents-and-media

Garcia-Molsosa, M., Collet-Sabé, J. and Montserrat, C. (2021). "Benefits, positive factors and difficulties perceived by mentors participating in a mentoring program aimed at youth in residential care", *Euro J Education*, Vol. 56, No. 3, pp. 496–510. doi:10.1111/ejed.12460

Henry, C., Wu, W., Moberg, K., Singer, S., Gabriel, B., Valente, R. et al. (2024). "Exploring inclusivity in entrepreneurship education provision: A European study", *Journal of Business Venturing Insights*, Vol. 22, e00494. doi:10.1016/j.jbvi.2024.e00494

Hooley, T., Hutchinson, J. and Neary, S. (2016). "Ensuring quality in online career mentoring", *British Journal of Guidance & Counselling*, Vol. 44, No. (1), pp. 26–41. doi:10.1080/03069885.2014.1002385

Kakouris, A. (2009). Online platforms for entrepreneurship education: An instructional design approach. In: *4th European Conference on Entrepreneurship and Innovation* (230–235) Belgium, September 2009.

Kakouris, A. (2017). Constructivist entrepreneurial teaching: The TeleCC online approach in Greece. In: Paul Jones, Gideon Maas und Luke Pittaway (Hg.): Entrepreneurship Education, Bd. 7. Emerald Publishing Limited (Contemporary Issues in Entrepreneurship Research), pp. 235–258.

Kaufmann, D. and Malul, M. (2015). "The dynamic brain drain of entrepreneurs in peripheral regions", *European Planning Studies*, Vol. 23, No. 7, pp. 1345–1356.

Lall, Saurabh A.; Chen, Li-Wei; Mason, Dyana P. (2022). "Digital platforms and entrepreneurial support: A field experiment in online mentoring", *Small Bus Econ*, Vol. 61, No. 4, pp. 631–654. doi:10.1007/s11187-022-00704-8

Lingelbach, D. (2005). The distinctiveness of entrepreneurship in developing countries. *UTSA College of Business Center for Global Entrepreneurship Working Paper No. 1*

Mazzarol, T., Battisti, M. and Clark, D. (2016). The role of universities as catalysts within entrepreneurial ecosystems. In "Rhetoric and reality: Building vibrant and sustainable entrepreneurial ecosystems by Delwyn Clark, Tui McKeown, Martina Battisti (pp.36-68). Tilde University Press

Miller, P. and Wendell-Wedellsborg, T. (2013). "*Innovation as usual: How to help your people bring great ideas to life*". Harvard Business Review Press.

Mouammer, L. and Bazan, C. (2021). "Effect of mentorship on the early entrepreneurial journey of university students". In: PCEEA. doi:10.24908/pceea.vi0.14969

Mullen, C.A. (2021). "Online doctoral mentoring in a pandemic: Help or hindrance to academic progress on dissertations?", *IJMCE*, Vol. 10, No. 2, pp. 139–157. doi:10.1108/ijmce-06-2020-0029

Nabi, G., Walmsley, A., and Akhtar, I. (2021). "Mentoring functions and entrepreneur development in the early years of university", *Studies in Higher Education*, Vol. 46, No. 6, pp. 1159–1174. doi:10.1080/03075079.2019.1665009

Naudé, W. (2013). "Entrepreneurship and economic development: Theory, evidence and policy". IZA Discussion Paper No. 7507. July 2013

Rechter, E. and Avnimelech, G. (2024). "Intensive personal mentoring: Accelerators' secret sauce", *Small Business Economics*, Vol. 64. 1259–1284. https://doi.org/10.1007/s11187-024-00943-x

Rigg, C. and O'Dwyer, B. (2012). "Becoming an entrepreneur: Researching the role of mentors in identity construction", *Education + Training*, Vol. 54, No. 4, pp. 319–329. doi:10.1108/00400911211236181

Russell, L. (2007). "Mentoring is not for you!: Mentee voices on managing their mentoring experience", *Improving Schools*, Vol. 10, No. 1, pp. 41–52. doi:10.1177/1365480207073721

Sarri, K.K. (2011). "Mentoring female entrepreneurs: A mentors' training intervention evaluation", *Journal of European Industrial Training*, Vol. 35, No. 7, pp. 721–741. doi:10.1108/03090591111160814

Seet, P.-S., Jones, J., Oppelaar, L. and Corral de Zubielqui, G. (2018). "Beyond 'know-what' and 'know-how' to 'know-who': Enhancing human capital with social capital in an Australian start-up accelerator",

Asia Pacific Business Review, Vol. 24, No. 2, pp. 233–260. doi:10.1080/13602381.2018.1431250

Singer-Coudoux, K., Buxmann, H. and Will, M. (2024). "Empowering future entrepreneurs: Developing an online entrepreneurial mentoring program across diverse EU regions", *European Conference on Innovation and Entrepreneurship*, Vol. 19, pp. 721–728. doi:10.34190/ecie.19.1.2599

Stam, E. and van de Ven, A. (2021). "Entrepreneurial ecosystem elements", *Small Business Economics*, Vol. 56, No. 2, pp. 809–832. doi:10.1007/s11187-019-00270-6

St-Jean, E., Radu-Lefebvre, M. and Mathieu, C. (2018). "Can less be more? Mentoring functions, learning goal orientation, and novice entrepreneurs' self-efficacy", *International Journal of Entrepreneurial Behavior & Research*, Vol. 24, No. 1, pp. 2–21. doi:10.1108/ijebr-09-2016-0299

Walsh, K. (2016). "Online mentoring in medical education", *South African Family Practice*, Vol. 58 (supl), pp. S7–S8. doi:10.1080/20786190.2015.1059020

Xie, Y. (2024). "Research On the uneven distribution of educational resources in China", *Journal of Education, Humanities and Social Sciences*, pp. 86–91. doi:10.54097/m2x54q97

5 Entrepreneurship education to foster innovation

The role of hackathons

Contributors: Katerina Zargani, Nektaria Berikou, Nikos Vogiatzis, Jorge-A. Sanchez-P from Corallia, Paola Belingheri, and Christian Lechner from LUISS

5.1 Hackathons as innovation drivers

The hackathon phenomenon has emerged as an effective approach to encouraging innovation with digital technologies in a wide range of sectors. Evolving from impromptu pizza parties and developing into bespoke corporate team-building events, hackathons have grown in a global way.

A hackathon is typically defined as a time-bound competitive event where participants collaborate to build proofs of concept and minimum viable products for a specific pre-defined problem or to innovate. Each team has to deliver a presentation (a PowerPoint, pitch for a quick demonstration of their solution for a specific challenge/topic). In fact, the term hackathon is a combination of "hack" and "marathon." The word "hack" refers to the idea that knowledge and information sharing should be seen positively while "marathon" refers to the intense, non-stop period dedicated to developing a prototype (Emmanouil et al., 2024.

Over time, "hackathons" have come to describe many kinds of time-limited creation events, often corporate, technical and non-technical, in-person and virtual, aiming to support open innovation and creativity. This has led to the rise of hackathon events, which are considered to have had a significant impact on the culture of digital innovation (Heller et al., 2023).

Hackathons have been extensively studied as facilitators of innovation. They offer numerous benefits to both organizers and participants. Hackathons can empower start-ups by fostering creativity, skill

DOI: 10.4324/9781003607649-6

development, and networking. Furthermore, they accelerate innovation by initiating and speeding up novel processes, generating a wealth of ideas, and identifying emerging talent. Hackathons also provide opportunities to integrate external knowledge, broadening perspectives and stimulating creativity. Ultimately, they contribute to an organization's public image by showcasing its commitment to innovation and broadening the innovation landscape (Angarita and Nolte, 2020). According to Nolte et al. (2020), hackathons, data dives, codefests, hack-days, sprints, and edit-a-thons have gained a great deal of attention from both practitioners and researchers.

The hackathon format significantly influences the overall experience, ultimately impacting participants, time, programming, and materials. While the format of each hackathon may vary to fit a certain context, make the most of local opportunities, better involve local multipliers and stakeholders, and engage participants, hackathons are based on a standard structure. Each hackathon is estimated to last between 2 and 5 days, during which individuals gather and form collocated teams intending to complete a project of interest (Chau et al., 2023).

An integral part of the hackathon experience is the people who participate. Hackathon participants, often called "hackers," are the lifeblood. Hackers are individuals encouraged to form teams or work independently on projects to develop solutions. Other important roles include mentors, who provide technical or project management expertise and guidance, impacted stakeholders, staff (paid), volunteers (unpaid), and judges. In traditional competitive hackathons, judges—often representatives from corporate sponsors, university professors, and domain experts—are responsible for selecting winning projects (Chau et al., 2023).

Hackathons may or may not have a theme.

- **Themed hackathons** focus on a specific aspect of human activity or value (e.g., "sustainability" or "future innovation"), a specific market (e.g., "transportation," "space," "insurance"), and/or a specific technology to use (e.g., requiring participants to focus on AI solutions or data and signals coming from satellite systems). Themed hackathons tend to identify a specific set of challenges to be taken on by participants. Nonthemed hackathons, on the other hand, may be completely open to any idea and may have no challenges at all.

- **Nonthemed hackathons** are extremely rare and have the disadvantage of making it hard for participants to identify a project to focus on without much external input. Choosing a theme is very important in order to attract the right audience. Identifying concrete challenges is strongly recommended. Challenges should be formulated in a way that helps participants identify a specific problem or group of problems, without constraining them too much and leaving no space for creativity and differentiation. Depending on the purpose of the hackathon, the challenges may be announced way ahead of the hackathon dates or during the opening ceremony of the hackathon.

Depending on the scale, the regional focus of hackathons may differ. In general, hackathons may be local, national, or international. International hackathons consist of several local or national hackathons that take place at (approximately) the same time and follow a common framework. International hackathons may have geographic restrictions of their own, taking place only in, for example, a given Region or Country (such as the Balkans) or between EU member countries (e.g., the CASSINI Hackathons) or be truly global (such as the NASA Space Apps Challenge).

Hackathons are usually not limited to the main competition event but are a long process offering all necessary support for ideas to be transformed into mature products and services and for teams to flourish in successful start-ups. They often involve warmup sessions, training, and workshops prior to the competition, allowing for creating stronger bonds among team members and a deeper understanding of the challenges. But even during the main event, achieving sustainable outcomes requires a blend of hacking and training (Teuberer, 2017).

While some hackathons may focus solely on the competition, many are structured with a continuation phase to help projects progress beyond the event. Overlooking the potential for project continuation can be a missed opportunity for both organizers and participants, as continued support has numerous benefits. After the hackathon, one best practice is to support winners with targeted growth programs that include further training, mentoring, and access to a network of high-profile mentors, all with the aim of transforming ideas into successful start-ups (Nolte et al., 2020).

5.1.1 The impact of hackathons

Hackathons can have a major impact on start-ups. They offer numerous benefits, such as networking opportunities, skill development, and the rapid prototyping of ideas. Hackathons mirror the open-innovation model by promoting teamwork, external partnerships, and rapid problem-solving.

Rexhepi et al. (2019) emphasized the value of diverse partnerships in boosting innovation performance. By engaging with a wide range of interdisciplinary partners, start-ups can inspire creativity and develop innovative solutions. In fact, the study found that this effect is stronger for high-tech start-ups. Their research significantly contributes to our understanding of how open innovation can enhance entrepreneurship, highlighting the importance of diverse knowledge and showing how this type of knowledge and partnerships can drive start-up success. Hackathons align with this idea by bringing together individuals from different fields to tackle shared challenges, expanding the potential for innovation among participating start-ups.

Hackathons offer numerous benefits to start-ups and university teams, including increased visibility, enhanced credibility, and accelerated innovation. By fostering collaboration and tapping into a wider pool of expertise, hackathons can help teams overcome limitations and develop innovative solutions. To assess the impact of a hackathon, it is essential to consider the entire result chain: **outputs, outcomes, and impact**. While outcomes represent the immediate changes resulting from a hackathon, impact speaks to the long-term effects and societal benefits. Sustainable impact means that the positive effects of a hackathon must endure over time. While completing the event is a significant achievement, it is crucial to focus on the lasting impact of the generated outcomes. Measuring impact involves evaluating the outcomes and assessing their causal relationship with the observed effects, considering various metrics, such as user adoption, revenue generation, or social impact (Emmanouil et al., 2024).

5.1.2 Key factors for successful hackathons

Recognized as a powerful tool for open innovation and inspiring entrepreneurial intentions, hackathons underscore the need for open data and investment, which are essential for success and for promoting start-up development. However, studies have shown that many hackathon projects often are not completed. To address this issue, it can be helpful to engage entrepreneurs and venture capitalists as jurors. These jurors can assess the potential of projects and connect developers with investors.

In their study, Soltani et al. (2016) identified six critical factors that organizers need to take into consideration to ensure the success of hackathons. These factors came out of interviews with the involved parties during various hackathon competitions. The six factors are as follows:

1) *A clearly defined scope.* Identifying concrete challenges helps participants identify a specific problem or group of problems without constraining them too much and leaving no space for creativity and differentiation.
2) *Offering rewards to winning teams can be a strong motivator for participation.* Tangible rewards like prizes or gifts often attract more participants.
3) *Team diversity is essential for innovation.* Collaboration among team members with diverse competencies, skills, and backgrounds can spark creativity and lead to more innovative solutions.
4) *Mentors* play a pivotal role in guiding and supporting participants. Mentors should share their knowledge and expertise to help hackers develop innovative solutions.
5) *Jury knowledge* is essential for ensuring a fair evaluation process. The sixth factor has to do with clearly defined eligibility requirements to ensure a competition runs smoothly and efficiently. These factors create a structured and supportive environment that fosters innovation and effective problem-solving during hackathons.

An additional key factor for a successful hackathon is the inclusion of training workshops and seminars. These sessions can be invaluable for introducing newcomers to hackathon themes or specific technical skills relevant to the competition. Training seminars or hands-on workshops offer newcomers a more comfortable entry point, providing a structured learning experience before diving into the hacking phase (Kamariotou and Kitsios, 2022).

5.2 ENTREPRENEDU's hackathons: a case study

In the framework of the ENTREPRENEDU project, a series of three hackathons were held in Italy, Greece, and Bulgaria. These three different locations ensured a diverse mix of participants, stakeholders, industries, sectors, and generated solutions. The entities responsible for overseeing the hackathons were three organizations with vast experience in planning similar events: Fondazione E. Amaldi (Italy), Corallia (Greece), and Cleantech Bulgaria (Bulgaria).

To maintain alignment across the ENTREPRENEDU hackathons, Corallia took the lead in overall coordination, leveraging its extensive experience in designing, promoting, and organizing these types of events while ensuring the relevance at European, national, and regional levels. An overall framework and specific guidelines were established to facilitate this coordination across the different locations.

HackTheBusiness served as an entrepreneurship challenge for young minds to learn, explore and discover the secrets of the DeepTech industry. The competition encouraged participants to think outside of the box, refining their pitches and leveraging their creativity. HackTheBusiness events were the perfect opportunity for young individuals and start-ups to present their business concepts to a panel of esteemed judges and industry leaders and get invited to the ENTREPRENEDU Mentoring & Coaching Program, where they could receive all the support needed to level-up their business idea.

Throughout the competitions, participants received support from mentors and attended a total of 16 workshops, which enabled the three HackTheBusiness events to generate a total of 94 business ideas. Out of these 94 business ideas, 13 winners (four from the first two events and five from the last one) were asked to participate in an exclusive 60-hour mentoring and business acceleration program where experts from the ENTREPRENEDU consortium provided entrepreneurial training on several topics, incorporating best practices from the events to support them going forward.

Though the format of each hackathon varied to fit the context, make the most of local opportunities, better involve local multipliers and stakeholders, and engage participants, all three hackathons were based on a common structure, consisting of the four main stages described below:

- Planning and design
- Campaign—information sessions
- Launch
- Hackathon event

5.2.1 Planning and design

The first step in designing the ENTREPRENEDU hackathons involved identifying their scope: the extent of the area to which the hackathon is relevant. The scope of each hackathon (or of any other similar initiative) can be analyzed through these interlinked factors: *purpose*, *scale*, *openness*, *context*, *target groups,* and *time frame*.

- **Purpose:** In the case of ENTREPRENEDU, the three hackathons followed the overall purpose of the project: "... creating a highly replicable and scalable education model (venture capital program) for both businesses and educational systems via a series of 3 Hackathons, developed at the regional level and supporting developed concepts and ideas to become concrete solutions".
- **Scale:** Depending on their scale, the regional focus of the hackathons differed. In general terms, hackathons could be local, national, or international.
  In the case of ENTREPRENEDU, three different regional hackathons took place (in three different countries focusing on their own regions) on different dates and with a possibly differing frameworks (though all directed towards fulfilling the purpose of the ENTREPRENEDU project).
- **Openness:** In terms of openness, hackathons are generally split into internal and external options. Internal hackathons focus on the personnel or community of the organizer (company, university, etc.). External ones, on the other hand, are more open to the public, accepting (or even focusing only on) external participants.

In the case of ENTREPRENEDU, the three hackathons were open to the broader public. HackTheBusiness targeted students, new start-ups, and researchers interested in acquiring entrepreneurial skills and exploring their business potential. Participants were challenged to propose revolutionary business ideas that could lead to successful start-ups. The competitions were open to EU residents aged 18–40 and primarily intended for on-site participation. Contestants could compete individually or in teams of up to six members.

Choosing a theme is typically very important to attract the right audience. Identifying concrete challenges is strongly recommended. Challenges should be designed to guide participants in identifying a specific problem or set of problems while allowing enough flexibility to foster creativity and diverse solutions. Depending on the purpose of the hackathon, the challenges may be announced way ahead of the hackathon dates or during the opening ceremony (see comment on "lead time" in the next sub-section).

Context: The three ENTREPRENEDU hackathons each had a theme and challenges. However, all were aligned with the project's purpose and focused on a context that could enable the proliferation of new business models and entrepreneurial skills and the commercialization of the developed solutions.

Target group: The last aspect to be considered for the complete definition of a hackathon's scope is its target group(s). Identifying their characteristics is very important for setting specific hackathon registration eligibility criteria. These criteria may pertain to the potential participants' nationality, age, background, skills, and more. A hackathon may aim to attract aspiring entrepreneurs, innovators, and programmers. In this context, ENTREPRENEDU specifically targeted participants from Italy, Bulgaria, and Greece, aged 18–30.

Time frame: When it comes to the timing of a hackathon, for thorough and effective planning, three aspects must be taken into consideration:

- The **duration**
- The "**when**"
- The **timing**

In addition to the time-related aspects for the ENTREPRENEDU hackathons, space-related matters were of utmost importance for the success of the three events. The ENTREPRENEDU hackathons were mostly onsite events. Each ENTREPRENEDU local organizer selected the most appropriate format to maximize participation and the impact of the ENTREPRENEDU event.

The successful organization and facilitation of the ENTREPRENEDU hackathons required an enthusiastic and skilled team of members with complementary talents and capable leadership. All ENTREPRENEDU partners had active involvement in the organization and implementation of the hackathons (during planning and/or during the actual event) to achieve good results and ensure the successful planning of all three ENTREPRENEDU hackathons.

5.2.2 Organizers, sponsors, and jury

The local organizer for the ENTREPRENEDU hackathon carefully considered and assigned the following roles and task forces/teams when distributing responsibilities among ENTREPRENEDU partners:

- **Management and networking team**: The team oversaw the overall management of the hackathon, including coordinating the other organizer teams responsible for its facilitation. It was also responsible for seamless communication and alignment with other core activities of the organizing entity (e.g., European projects undertaken, entrepreneurship initiatives like incubators, etc.). This team put into place the overall strategy, management, and monitoring and evaluation tools necessary for successful hackathon implementation. Finally, the team focused on securing endorsements and support from governmental and public agencies, along with financial or in-kind contributions from sponsors.
- **Administration and financials team**: The team was responsible for all activities related to the preparation of the logistical part of the hackathon (venue, equipment, connectivity, catering, procurement, security, public hygiene, etc.) as well as the financials pertaining to the hackathon in general, such as budget estimation and monitoring, running all activities for receiving the sponsorships secured by the management and networking team, transferring monetary prizes to the local winners, etc. The team also managed and coordinated any volunteers that supported the hackathon on site.
- **Communications and marketing team**: The team was responsible for all activities related to branding, marketing, and communications for the hackathon and for attracting individuals and teams to participate in the event. It ran offline and online promotional activities, built and managed a network of community partners, and secured media and promotional sponsorships, etc.
- **Scientific and technical team**: The team was responsible for working on hackathon challenges and tailoring them to the local ecosystem's needs and interests, managing the scientific committee, the mentor and keynote speaker network, and the hackathon jury, creating guides for the hackathon participants, aggregating potential tools and datasets that could be used by aspiring hackers, etc.
- **Operations team:** This team was responsible for the hacker experience at the event. Everything having to do with the "look and feel"

of the hackathon was managed by this team. It also managed all hackathon platforms and facilitated pre-hackathon activities (e.g., team matchmaking).

Obviously, the task forces differed depending on the nature of each local organizer and each ENTREPRENEDU hackathon. It must be pointed out that all of the ENTREPRENEDU hackathon organizers' teams were aligned before the hackathon so that they could work as a unit rather than as distinct teams with different goals.

ENTREPRENEDU's hackathon involved a number of sponsors to achieve higher results and attract a larger audience. Five categories of sponsors were targeted based on the needs of each local organizer:

- **Financial sponsors**: These sponsors provided direct economic support to cover hackathon costs.
- **In-Kind sponsors**: Entities (usually companies) that provided free services or products, such as platform credits or hardware.
- **Strategic/media partners:** Entities that helped with marketing and promotion, frequently through publications and outreach-related activities.
- **Community partners:** Entities that assisted with free hacking, mentoring, judging, access to target events, or volunteer recruitment.

The ENTREPRENEDU hackathon jury committee consisted of consortium members, though external stakeholders were sometimes invited. In terms of the number of judges, usually about 5–7 members were involved (an odd number was chosen to deadlock situations). Moreover, if the external jury members had access to sensitive materials, they were asked to sign a confidentiality agreement. Finally, organizers worked to avoid any kind of conflict of interest between jury members and the teams in the competition.

5.2.3 Prehackathon campaign: promotion

The promotion of each hackathon followed the standard branding, marketing, and communications practices of the ENTREPRENEDU initiative.

Registration took place via an online platform provided by F6S and was available through the ENTREPENEDU project website.

Participants could register individually or as pre-established teams, indicating their skills to help balance team profiles. The organizers selected up to 80 participants for the hackathon, aiming for gendering diversity. Ineligible applicants were still encouraged to participate virtually by following keynote addresses, workshops streamed live on social media during the event's key moments, and the final pitch session with awards.

The promotional campaign for all three events was primarily conducted by F6S and included the following activities:

- **Website**: F6S created dedicated webpages for each competition, serving as central hubs for vital information such as competition details, agendas, and registration portals. This streamlined approach facilitated seamless navigation for participants, enhancing their overall experience and fostering greater interaction with the event.
- **Registration management**
- **Event platform**: The corresponding core organizer managed a dedicated event platform for each hackathon. The platform included valuable information required for potential participants to learn about the competition and the corresponding registration form.
- **Promotional materials**: Comprehensive promotional materials were created in order to maximize engagement, including dynamic content tailored to different platforms (LinkedIn, Facebook, and YouTube) and audiences, ensuring broad awareness and participation.
- **Press releases:** A variety of press releases were published on the official ENTREPRENEDU website.

Additionally, the ENTREPRENEDU team jointly collaborated to increase visibility and outreach by leveraging their extensive reach and expertise. Each entity ran their own dissemination campaigns (social media, press releases, articles, newsletters etc.) to engage more participants.

5.2.4 Pre-event activities

Before each competition, organizers prepared a comprehensive handbook for participants, available to be downloaded from the website. Different handbooks for each competition phase and target group (local organizers, participants, stakeholders, potential community partners/sponsors) were drafted and distributed (for a total of six handbooks) throughout the hackathons. These handbooks provided comprehensive information about each competition, including details about organization, preparation, event logistics, prizes, and other resources for successful participation in the competition.

Organizers held dedicated warm-up sessions prior to the events as part of the prehackathon campaign to promote the hackathons and attract participants.

During these sessions, participants had the opportunity to meet the organizing team virtually, ask questions, and delve into the intricacies of the competition. The event proved highly successful, offering all attendees a deep dive into the ENTREPRENEDU world, encouraging them to form teams with fellow members. The goal of each session was not only to attract potential participants but also to train them and provide highlights about the market and the technologies related to the topic of the hackaton. Overall, the sessions offered participants invaluable information, expert tips, and profound insights in preparation for the upcoming competitions.

Following each event, engaging Q&A sessions facilitated networking opportunities and allowed participants to ask questions and seek clarifications from organizers. Additionally, winners of previous hackathons shared their inspiring stories on how they transformed their ideas into successful start-ups. Finally, keynote speeches enriched the experience, offering strategic perspectives and fostering a deeper understanding of the industry landscape.

5.2.5 Hackathon event

The hacking period is the heart of the hackathon and the moment when teams focus on their mission, which is to create something novel and impactful. Teams concentrate on outlining their proposal, designing and offering an initial prototype, and describing their solution in an appealing way. The event should be seen as an opportunity for teams to document and demonstrate a solution rapidly by producing a prototype and/or rehearsing a pitch.

From the local organizer's side, the main activities during this period include:

- Supporting **matchmaking and team formation**.
- **Communicating timelines** and **rules** for every step of the hacking process—brainstorming, pitching, formulation, and presenting, including meal/coffee times.

Table 5.1 Topics covered in the training workshop

Session
Building future-proofed business ideas
Understanding business angels—fundraising tips for start-up founders
Business model discovery
From Idea to impact: Unlocking the potential of your business concepts
Entrepreneurship in space
How to apply to European Space Agency business incubation centers

Source: Contributors' own work.

- Making sure mentors/advisors are available to the participants and helping teams create their pitches.
- **Engaging participants** in other side activities (optional and, in some cases, counterproductive).
- Ensuring all participants have dedicated time to work on their projects and suitable physical or virtual space and equipment.

The ENTREPRENEDU team offered a series of training workshops throughout the hackathons. These workshops provided participants with in-depth knowledge and analysis in terms of developing entrepreneurial ecosystems tailored to regional innovation levels and specific needs. The main topics covered are presented in Table 5.1.

5.2.6 The competition

During the competition, all teams had to submit a presentation—a pitch deck (in PowerPoint or PDF format)—by the set deadline. A template was provided that outlined further details on the content to be included in the presentation. A demonstration/technical implementation related to the final presentation was optional.

The presentation followed this outline:

- **Introduction**: A summary of what you are going to present. Open with a simple statement such as "This is our team, and this is what we do."
- **Problem**: Description of the problem that you are trying to remedy or the opportunity that you want to take advantage of. Avoid looking for a solution that is searching for a problem.

- **Solution**: Explain how you will resolve the problem and the value that you will create. It is not necessary to provide an in-depth technical explanation. Merely provide the gist of how you will fix the problem (but do make sure that your idea is feasible).
- **Market**: Explain who the customers are or speak about the consumers you are targeting. Quantify the market (e.g., How big is it, in monetary terms?).
- **Business/pricing model**: Explain how you can make money—who will pay you, what are the channels of distribution you are going to use, what are your gross margins, etc.
- **Competition**: Are there alternatives? Are there direct or indirect competitors? Briefly categorize them.
- **Unique selling point(s):** Describe what makes you different from the competition.
- **Team:** Present the skills and roles of your team members. Identify why you are the team to solve the problem.
- **Timeline**: What are the next steps you can take to implement your idea? Are there any milestones?
- **Financials:** Present the expected costs, required funding you would need to make your idea a reality, and your expected revenues (projections/estimations).

5.2.7 Results and evaluation

Beyond the presentation submission, the teams had to pitch their idea and present it within a specific time period in front of a jury. Following all pitches, the teams were evaluated based on the criteria specified below, including innovation, feasibility, market scalability, and social impact.

The evaluation criteria included the following elements:

- **Technical innovation:** Is the idea innovative? Does it rely on technology transfer? Does it have the potential to secure Intellectual Property Rights (IPRs)?
- **Market attractiveness:** Does the idea address a real problem? Is there a market for it?
- **Business viability:** Is the business model sound? Can a company built around the presented idea run a successful business?
- **Investor interest:** Overall, can the idea attract interest from potential investors?

- **Funding opportunities:** Does the idea have the potential to secure funding from other sources (beyond investors), such as grants?
- **Educational impact:** Does the business/idea have a (side-)effect on education? Can people be trained/educated through it?
- **Team quality:** Is this the team to solve the problem?
- **Branding and marketing:** Has the team worked on its values, its branding, and its marketing (e.g., name selection for business/product, logo creation, graphics, creative content, etc.).

HackTheBusiness Italy had a total of 43 applications with 30 business ideas—five were from already formed teams, six came from start-ups, while the remaining number came from individuals. Eleven teams submitted their ideas for final evaluation and four winners were selected.

HackTheBusiness Greece received a total of 108 applications and 35 business ideas, with members from 4 different universities in Greece. Twelve teams competed in the finals, and four winners were selected.

HackTheBusiness Bulgaria received a total of 61 applications and 29 business ideas. Five winners were selected from a pool of 23 entries.

Table 5.2 shows the full list of events that have been organized under the ENTREPRENEDU Hackaton initiative.

Table 5.2 ENTREPRENEDU hackathons: Information about the main events

Competition	*Date*	*Theme*	*Business ideas*	*Finalists*	*Workshops during the hackathon*
Rimini, Italy	15–17/06/2023	DeepTech	30	4	6
Athens, Greece	25/11/2023	Space	35	4	5
Sofia, Bulgaria	26–27/03/2024	Sustainability	29	5	5

Source: Contributors' own work.

5.3 The HackTheBusiness competitions

5.3.1 HackTheBusiness Italy

HackTheBusiness Italy was held in Rimini during the "We Make Future 2023" event (June 15 to 17, 2023), the largest digital innovation fair in Italy. A dedicated space was reserved for hacking, workshops, and pitches, making this the perfect opportunity to hold the HackTheBusiness competition.

We Make Future has become synonymous with innovation, technology, and entrepreneurial spirit. This prestigious event attracts forward-thinking individuals from a variety of industries, offering a unique opportunity to explore emerging trends, network with industry experts, and gain invaluable insights. Figure 5.1 shows the logo of the HackTheBusiness Italy initiative.

HackTheBusiness Italy included 43 applications and **30 business ideas**. The aim of the hackathon was to bring together young talents and new entrepreneurs passionate about or interested in DeepTech with experts in business and innovation. The idea was to work together to develop innovative solutions enabled by DeepTech to address the needs of industry and society.

E. Amaldi Foundation was responsible for all aspects of the Italian hackathon: logistics, strategic stakeholder engagement, defining the challenge, developing the guide for participants, and evaluation board management.

Participants were invited to propose DeepTech business ideas representing a true revolution for the food, climate, and space industries.

Figure 5.1 HackTheBusiness Italy. Logo.
Source: ENTREPRENEDU.

The description of the challenges is provided below.

Challenge SPACE: This challenge sought business ideas that leveraged satellite data and space technologies to solve problems across various industries (energy, transportation, agriculture, etc.). The focus was on using space data and AI to analyze large datasets and create innovative solutions. It also highlighted the need for innovation in the space sector itself, such as new satellites and components. The aim of this challenge was to propose a business idea that addressed one or more of the issues facing the space sector.

Challenge FOOD: This challenge was about business ideas that used new technologies (AI, Blockchain, IoT) to create a more sustainable food system. The goal was to address issues like food security, reducing the environmental impacts from farming, and minimizing resource waste.

Challenge CLIMATE: This challenge sought out ideas that utilized emerging technologies to mitigate and adapt to climate change. Examples included intelligent forecasting systems, monitoring carbon neutrality, planning renewable energy grids, and protecting people from extreme weather events.

Before the competition, E. Amaldi Foundation prepared a comprehensive handbook for participants, available to be downloaded from the website. This handbook contained valuable information, such as the event timeline, agenda, eligibility criteria, stakeholder information, prizes, and other helpful details necessary for successful participation in the competition.

Amaldi Foundation, with the support of FS6, organized a warm-up session on May 30, 2023, as part of the prehackathon campaign in order to promote the events and attract participants. During this session, participants had the opportunity to meet the organizing team virtually, ask questions, and to delve into the intricacies of the competition. It attracted 28 attendees.

Over the 3 days of the competition, participants collaborated intensively with mentors to review their business ideas and think about potential gaps that might need to be filled. There was a great deal of pressure as each team aimed to deliver a concise, persuasive pitch highlighting their vision, value proposition, and market potential. To support their DeepTech development, participants also had the opportunity to attend workshops led by ENTREPRENEDU experts, gaining valuable business insights and practical tips. There were eight workshop sessions in total, covering different insightful topics:

- Business model discovery
- Spark your success: Unleashing the brilliance within your ideas
- Building future-proofed business ideas
- Understanding business angels—fundraising tips for start-ups
- From idea to impact: Unlocking the potential of your business concepts
- Entrepreneurship in space
- How to apply to the European Space Agency business incubation centers
- Useful tools for DeepTech business in Europe

After 3 days of intense work, excitement, learning, and fun, the ENTREPRENEDU team of experts selected the top four winning teams and their innovative DeepTech ideas. The winning teams were: BACKWARDS, SHADES OF BLUE, AS YOU LIKE, and BOBIS. They all demonstrated innovation and drive. BACKWARDS aimed to solve the problem of packaging waste by creating reusable packaging and logistics infrastructure while SHADES OF BLUE wanted to create a certification system and consultancy systems for the sustainable management of water resources, providing companies with monitoring, improving the negative impact on rivers and water. AS YOU LIKE set out to transform the dining experience with a mobile app that lets users customize meals, access real-time nutrition information with visual AI, and discover restaurants aligned with specific dietary needs. BOBIS proposed reducing CO2 emissions caused by last-mile logistics, offering the end user a platform to encourage local consumption while searching for products and services within three kilometers.

5.3.2 HackTheBusiness Greece

The second HackTheBusiness competition organized by the ENTREPRENEDU team was held in Greece in November 2024, where emerging talents gathered to showcase their groundbreaking space ideas. Figure 5.2 shows the logo of HackTheBusiness Greece initiative.

HackTheBusiness Greece was the first entrepreneurship and educational ideation contest that took place on a national level. The aim was to bring together young entrepreneurs with business and innovation experts to work together and develop innovative solutions enabled by DeepTech to address the needs of industry and society.

Figure 5.2 HackTheBusiness Greece. Logo.
Source: ENTREPRENEDU.

The HackTheBusiness Greece competition was planned by Corallia, with the support of the European Space Agency Business Incubation Center Greece (ESA BIC Greece), the Greek Space Technologies and Applications Cluster (si-Cluster), the STARTAB Entrepreneurship Program. It was under the auspices of the Ministry of Digital Governance with four co-organizers: National Technical University of Athens, the University of Thessaly, the Aristotle University of Thessaloniki and the Democritus University of Thrace.

HackTheBusiness Greece consisted of two phases. During the first phase, four different local competitions (physical events) took place simultaneously in different cities all over Greece in collaboration with local Universities (Athens, Thessaloniki, Volos, Xanthi). During the second phase (the finals), winners of each local competition gathered in Athens, where they pitched their ideas against each other.

As the main organizer, Corallia was responsible for all related activities (logistics, strategic stakeholders, and sponsor engagement, defining the challenges, and developing several guides—local organizers, jury, participants, and evaluation board management.

The main theme of the competition was "**space.**" Specifically, participants were invited to:

- identify a problem/challenge faced by the space industry and provide a solution based on pre-existing or new space technology and/or systems.

- introduce a product or service based on a transfer of space technology to, and/or the utilization of, a space system in a non-space environment (spin-off). For example, the participants could suggest using images from Earth observation satellites to create a new precision agriculture application.
- facilitate the use of nonspace technology in the space market (spin-in). For instance, the participants could suggest introducing blockchain technology (originally coming from the logistics/financial sector) in managing satellite clusters.

In other words, any innovative idea was considered acceptable as long as "space" was either the origin of the challenge or the basis of the solution.

Educational entities (Democritus University of Thrace, National Technical University of Athens, Aristotle University of Thessaloniki, and the University of Thessaly) played a crucial role in the planning of the first phase of the HackTheBusiness Greece, acting as local organizers. This enabled universities to reinforce their position as hubs of education and innovation, engage with their local ecosystems, and identify new space challenges and solutions. The competition also served as a milestone for future activities, further solidifying their involvement in the Greek space sector.

The first phase of the event was held from November 3–5, 2023, at four different universities across Greece: Democritus University of Thrace (DUTH); National Technical University of Athens (NTUA); Aristotle University of Thessaloniki (AUTH); and University of Thessaly (UTH). Teams with the most innovative ideas received mentoring and a paid ticket to the finals. The second phase of the competition—the finals—took place in Athens, Greece on November 25, 2023, at the Corallia premises. The HackTheBusiness Greece competition was a hybrid event. The first phase featured physical events in four locations, with workshops and one-on-one mentoring sessions conducted both online (discord used) and physically. The final event and awards ceremony included on-site participation from both organizers, participants, and speakers.

In the first phase, four different local competitions (physical events) took place simultaneously in four different cities in Greece in collaboration with the educational entities under the coordinated guidance of Corallia. During the 3-day local competitions, participants actively collaborated with mentors to refine their business ideas and win over the judges. Teams attended four workshops led by the ENTREPRENEDU team and sponsors, gaining valuable business insights. Furthermore, one-on-one sessions were organized between the hackathon teams and the mentors. These sessions focused on both technical and business aspects of the solutions, as well as on presentation tips and tricks.

The award ceremony was live-streamed across all four locations in Greece, with winners selected by local organizers in collaboration with Corallia.

In the first phase of the competition, a total of 68 participants, divided into 18 teams, participated.

During the local competition, all official communications were conducted over the Discord platform. Discord was utilized to connect mentors with participants and for teams to submit their project ideas. Events (e.g., the launch Session, and webinars) were also streamed via this platform.

5.3.3 HackTheBusiness Bulgaria

Cleantech Bulgaria hosted the final round of the ENTREPRENEDU HackTheBusiness Bulgaria, an entrepreneurial hackathon for students, young professionals, and early-stage start-ups.

HackTheBusiness Bulgaria was a golden opportunity for aspiring European entrepreneurs to step into the business world. Participants were invited to delve into the realms of sustainability and digitization, addressing challenges from diverse sectors. This dynamic business ideation competition provided a space for aspiring entrepreneurs to harness their creativity, collaborate with like-minded individuals, and bring their innovative ideas to life. HackTheBusiness Bulgaria counted a total of 61 applications with 29 business ideas. In a groundbreaking finale hosted by Cleantech Bulgaria, the third and final installment of the HackTheBusiness hackathon series sparked a wave of innovation set to redefine Europe's sustainable landscape.

With a sharp focus on green and eco-conscious solutions spanning agri-food, construction, manufacturing, and digital and creative industries, participants were primed to unleash their creativity and address pressing environmental challenges head-on. The goal was to catalyze contributions towards a future that's not only environmentally aware but also resilient across these pivotal sectors.

HackTheBusiness Bulgaria took place on March 26th and 27th at the Innovation Forum "John Atanasoff" of Sofia Tech Park, gathering

ENTREPRENEDU
Enhancing entrepreneurial ecosystems for education

HackTheBusiness
HACKATHON BULGARIA
26 & 27 March, Sofia

Figure 5.3 HackTheBusiness Bulgaria. Logo.
Source: ENTREPRENEDU.

young entrepreneurs, researchers, and early-stage start-ups to pitch innovative and sustainable business ideas. Hosted by Cleantech Bulgaria, this event aimed to transform the European sustainable ecosystem and resulted in a variety of eco-conscious solutions and ideas connected with agri-food, construction, manufacturing, and the digital and creative industries. Figure 5.3 shows the logo of the HackTheBusiness Bulgaria initiative.

Participants had the opportunity to network and gain valuable insights from industry mentors.

The HackTheBusiness Bulgaria competition was an on-site event. On the first day of the competition, participants had the opportunity to form teams, meet the mentors, and attend workshops carefully designed by the ENTREPRENEDU team in order to equip them with the necessary skills and knowledge to master their pitch decks. During the second day of the competition, each team had a brief 7-minute window to explain the vision and mission behind their solutions. After each pitching session, the teams answered questions from the jury committee. Following all pitches, the 12 teams were evaluated based on criteria specified, including innovation, feasibility, market scalability, and social impact.

The event concluded with a prestigious award ceremony where the winners and prizes were announced. Following the award ceremony, a networking cocktail event was held for all participants, partners, investors, political figures, and fellow attendees.

5.3.4 HackTheBusiness: phase two

Winners of the local competitions were invited to join the mentoring program offered by the Corallia team. This program provided winning teams with the opportunity to receive guidance from experienced mentors, who helped them refine their business ideas, enhance their expertise, and excel in the competition.

Following local competitions, winners from each region gathered in Athens on November 25, 2023, to pitch their innovative business ideas for a chance to join ENTREPRENEDU's business acceleration program, where promising ventures got the support needed to become a reality.

The final competition was held with the support of the Greek Ministry of Digital Governance, and the deputy minister was in attendance. Community partners and stakeholders actively took part in the final competition and shared their insights about space and entrepreneurship, while three successful start-up companies, participants in previous hackathons, shared their inspiring stories and journeys in becoming successful entrepreneurs. Afterwards, each team had a brief seven-minute window to explain the vision and mission behind their space solutions. After each pitching session, the teams answered questions from the jury committee. Following all pitches, the 12 teams were evaluated based on innovation, feasibility, market scalability, and social impact criteria.

The award ceremony followed with the announcement of the winners and prizes. The final event concluded with networking among all participants, partners, investors, and fellow attendees.

ENTREPRENEDU's HackTheBusiness initiative culminated in a resounding success, fostering innovation, and supporting young people in Europe. The overall satisfaction of participants in the ENREPRENEDU hackathons was high, making for a generally positive experience. All hackathons were well-received, with participants finding them valuable and offering relevant challenges and workshops. Most participants appreciated the collaborative atmosphere, valuable workshops, access to mentors, and, most importantly, the opportunity to innovate. Few participants highlighted the need for better organization and clearer communication regarding event logistics and expectations. The unique learning experiences and the networking opportunities provided were among the deciding factors.

Twelve winning teams, chosen from three hackathons held in Italy, Greece, and Bulgaria, have embarked upon the ENTREPRENEDU

Mentoring & Coaching Program. This targeted program equips young entrepreneurs with the essential knowledge and guidance to transform their innovative ideas into successful start-ups. The program's impact extends beyond the winners, as over 100 European participants actively took part in the hackathons. Participants showcased their creativity and technical prowess by developing solutions in the space, sustainability, and climate arenas.

5.4 Conclusions

The HackTheBusiness experience is more than just a competition—it's an immersive journey of learning and growth filled with business tips and tricks presented by ENTREPRENEDU experts. Every participant had the unparalleled opportunity to meet the panel of judges and mentors, receiving constructive feedback aimed at improving their ideas and strategies to perfection. Participants benefited from practical business tips and tricks designed to maximize hacking efficiency. Furthermore, the esteemed panel of judges and mentors offered invaluable feedback, helping participants refine their ideas and strategies to a competitive edge.

HackTheBusiness fostered a collaborative environment that pushed boundaries and sparked new business ideas. With this successful launch, ENTREPRENEDU paves the way for future hackathons to empower even more young minds across Europe.

References

Angarita, M.A., and Nolte, A. (2020) "What do we know about hackathon outcomes and how to support them? – A systematic literature review". In *International conference on collaboration technologies and social computing*, Vol. 1, pp 50–64.

Chau, C.W. and Gerber, E.M. (2023). "On hackathons: A multidisciplinary literature review." In *Proceedings of the 2023 CHI Conference on Human Factors in Computing Systems*, Hamburg, Germany, April.

Emmanouil, M., et al. (2024). "Maximising hackathon impact: A comprehensive framework for sustaining post-event outcome," *European Conference on Innovation and Entrepreneurship*, Vol. 19, No. 1, pp. 191–199.

Heller, B., Amir A., Waxman R. and Maaravi Y. (2023). "Hack your organizational innovation: Literature review and integrative model for running hackathons", *Journal of Innovation and Entrepreneurship*, Vol. 12, No. 1, pp 1–24.

Kamariotou, M. and Kitsios, F. (2022). "Hackathons for driving service innovation strategies: The evolution of a digital platform-based ecosystem", *Journal of Open Innovation: Technology, Market, and Complexity*, Vol. 8 No. 3, p. 111.

Nolte, A., Chounta, I.A. and Herbsleb, J.D. (2020). "What happens to all these hackathon projects? Identifying factors to promote hackathon project continuation", *Human-Computer Interaction*, Vol. 4, No. 145, pp 1–26.

Rexhepi, G., Hisrich, R.D. and Ramadani, V. (2019). "Open innovation and entrepreneurship: Impetus of growth and competitive advantages", Springer International Publishing, Cham.

Soltani, P.M., Pessi, K., Ahlin, K. and Wernered, I. (2014). "Hackathon: A method for digital innovative success: A comparative descriptive study." In *VIIIth European Conference on IS Management and Evaluation*, Ghent, Belgium, September.

Tauberer, J. (2017). How to run a successful hackathon. [Online]. Available at: https://hackathon.guide/ (Accessed: 15 November 2024).

For detailed information about the Cassini Hackathon format, visit: www.cassini.eu/hackathons/

For detailed information about the NASA Space Apps Challenge, visit: www.spaceappschallenge.org/

F6S is a global online community that helps founders and startups grow to solve the world's pressing social, economic, environmental, sustainability, and innovation problems. F6S members include the world's top companies, earlier stage companies, startups scaling towards unicorn status and other supporters. For more information visit: www.f6s.com/company/f6s#about

For detailed information about the Cassini Hackathon format, visit: www.cassini.eu/hackathons/

For detailed information about the NASA Space Apps Challenge, visit: www.spaceappschallenge.org/

F6S is a global online community that helps founders and startups grow to solve the world's pressing social, economic, environmental, sustainability, and innovation problems. F6S members include the world's top companies, earlier stage companies, startups scaling towards unicorn status and other supporters. For more information visit: www.f6s.com/company/f6s#about

6 New technological trends in entrepreneurship education

6.1 The role of digitalization and the new frontiers of digital learning for entrepreneurship

The advancement of digitalization and the progressive integration of digital technology into the working and living spaces of individuals is having a profound impact on education systems, generating new models of phygital research and teaching—that is, models that integrate physical (in-person) and digital activities. As a result, we are witnessing the emergence of the "digital university" model (Fernández et al., 2023).

An important accelerator of the adoption of new technologies in the education sector was the extraordinary event of the Covid-19 pandemic, which saw universities focus on online distance learning to ensure they could carry out their missions despite limitations to mobility and social interactions (Masalimova, 2022). When distance working and learning were imposed by the need to maintain social distancing, technology was crucial in ensuring continuous and flexible access to education (Akintayo et al., 2024).

Additionally, the growing number of entrepreneurial education offerings confirms the significance of and demand for focused educational courses at all levels of age and specialization. Focusing on higher and adult education, a wide range of courses, models, and frameworks has been offered and elaborated to guide entrepreneurial action and develop entrepreneurial mindset and competencies.

By educational tools, we focus on the resources or technologies designed to assist in the process of teaching and learning, such

DOI: 10.4324/9781003607649-7

as software applications, websites, educational games, interactive whiteboards, simulations, and other digital or physical resources that can be used to enhance the learning experience. Within the specific domain of entrepreneurial education, the tools have a specific focus on value creation, venture creation, and related entrepreneurial competencies such as scanning scenarios, team working, action, etc. These educational tools may range widely not only in term of methods, objectives and depth but also in rigor and relevance.

Methodologically, the use of educational tool is not new in entrepreneurial education, where frameworks methodologies an techniques are used throughout diverse entrepreneurial education approaches (Lackeus, 2015) such as, for example: (i) Effectuation (Sarasvathy, 2001; Sarasvathy and Dew, 2005; Sarasvathy and Venkataraman, 2011), that supports the use of existing resources, collaboration, and experimentation to support different stages of entrepreneurial action; (ii) Business modeling and canvasing and the related methods and tools (Osterwalder and Pigneur, 2010), that describe how to best develop the set of elements through which ventures may create, transfer to other parties, and at the same time capture the created values; (iii) Lean startup, and the need for tools and framework to quickly validate hypotheses of value creation people; or (iv) Design thinking and the use of techniques and tools to foster problem-solving activities, by reasoning, iterating, and creating meaning (Johansson-Sköldberg et al., 2013).

As the primary objective of educational tools is that of supporting the acquisition of knowledge and the development of competencies, they are usually integrated into traditional teaching and serve different purposes. In particular, educational technologies representing a growing area of tool development are defined as "Devices, apps, webs, resources, internet access, technology support and other digital tools used to deepen learning." (ISTE, 2017).

Beyond simply facilitating access, the use of new technologies in teaching and learning has been recognized for its role in improving educational outcomes, increasing student engagement and motivation, and enhancing the learning outcome (Criollo et al., 2023). In the context of entrepreneurship, it has also been found that digital entrepreneurship education has a positive impact on students' self-efficacy and their ability to create new business ventures in the digital domain (Wardoyo et al., 2025).

6.1.1 The rise of Edtech in entrepreneurship education

Digital technologies are radically altering the education landscape, redefining both teaching methods and learning strategies. In this context, the rise of the technologies for education, the so called "EdTech", has led to the introduction of interactive digital tools and the increasing hybridisation of learning environments, which has improved the accessibility and effectiveness of education (Chen et al., 2020); it has also fostered greater transparency, accountability, and efficiency in teaching processes (Rahmatullah et al., 2022). The relevance of edtech is demonstrated by the explosive growth of its market value, which is expected to reach $22.4 billion in 2025 from only $4 billion in 2018 (Eastern Peak, 2025).[1]

Among the most popular tools available on digital platforms are apps, discussion boards, digital assignments and video submissions, quizzes, surveys, collaborative workspaces, whiteboard responses, and various third-party programs and tools (Bradley, 2021).

Barbetta (2023) has categorized these technologies into four key online instructional methods: content presentations, game-based learning and gamification, peer collaboration, and multimedia. Each of these methods is designed to cater to different aspects of the learning experience, promoting engagement, knowledge retention, and meaningful participation in the learning process. In line with this framework, Table 6.1 provides an overview of the main usage of each technology for entrepreneurship education.

The characteristics of these tools also make them useful for creating new learning opportunities linked to entrepreneurship. Technologies integrated into learning environments can facilitate the transfer of entrepreneurial skills; enhance students' ability to innovate, collaborate, and communicate their ideas effectively in the digital economy, and support lifelong learning processes for upskilling and reskilling as well as promoting self-entrepreneurship (Hamilton, 2021).

When discussing edtech innovations, it is important to highlight blockchain technology. Blockchain's ability to streamline processes, increase data security, and reduce administrative burdens makes it an ideal tool for improving the efficiency of credentialing systems. By allowing for instant verification of academic records, it ensures that certificates, diplomas and achievements are tamper-proof.

Table 6.1 Main technologies and related use in entrepreneurial education

Technology	*Main use in entrepreneurship education*	*Short description*
Learning Management Systems (LMS)	Deliver and manage entrepreneurship courses	Platforms for organizing content, assignments, and communication in one digital space
Virtual classrooms	Support live, interactive online sessions	Tools for real-time teaching, discussions, and presentations in online or blended courses
Simulations and experiential tools	Develop entrepreneurial thinking through practice	Games, role-plays, and case studies that replicate real-world business challenges
Collaborative tools	Foster teamwork and peer learning	Platforms for group work, discussions, polls, and shared content creation
VR/AR and data visualization	Explore virtual business environments and interpret data visually	Immersive tools to simulate markets, visualize models, and analyze data
AI and adaptive learning	Personalize learning paths and automate support tasks	Technologies that adjust content to learners' needs and assist with course management

Source: author elaboration.

Furthermore, blockchain can offer more efficient tracking of students' learning progress, thus enabling the creation of a continuous and dynamic learning environment that adapts to the needs of both students and professionals. Table 6.2 presents an overview of the main active learning technologies.

6.1.2 Emerging technologies for digital mentoring

As part of the digitalization of entrepreneurship education, new forms of mentoring have emerged that are becoming more prevalent, with the online as a driver for interaction between mentor and mentee. By using digital platforms, remote mentoring allows increased access to entrepreneurs in remote geographical areas; this

Table 6.2 Online active-learning technologies

Technology	*Description*
Book Creator	Online platform for creating multimedia digital books concerning various subject areas
EdPuzzle	Online technology for faculty and students to add interactivity to videos by embedding questions, audio notes, audio tracks, or comments
Flip (formerly Flipgrid)	Online technology that develops grids with questions or topics to facilitate active learning. Students respond to the grid by making short videos for discussion boards or homework
Flippity	This tool lets faculty create active-learning games, memory games, word searches, board games, bingo games and more from templates using Google spreadsheets. The tool also has a leaderboard and badge-tracker tools
Gimkit	Digital game-based quiz that can be assigned for independent practice or used in a group interactive review game
Google Docs	Online tool that lets students collaboratively create and edit online documents in real time. It can be used for collaborative online note taking or writing projects
Google Jamboard	Online digital whiteboards for collaboration in a shared digital space. It can be used synchronously for brainstorming, problem-solving and more. Asynchronously, students can virtually gather on a video platform to discuss ideas as they map them
Google Sheets	Web-based application to collaboratively create and edit spreadsheets in real time or at different times
Guided Notes	Faculty-prepared skeletal outlines that can be used to take notes during online presentations and (asynchronously) from recorded faculty presentations
Kahoot	Online system with gamification elements used to create live quizzes, polls and more. Students can complete these quizzes and polls as teams synchronously or independently asynchronously

(*Continued*)

Table 6.2 (Continued)

Technology	*Description*
Linoit	Online digital bulletin board where students can virtually place sticky notes with text, videos or images individually or collaboratively across curricular areas
MindMeister	Collaborative, online mind-mapping tool to make connections among ideas, concepts, etc.
Mindomo	Online collaborative mind-mapping and concept-mapping program for collaborative brainstorming and making connections among concepts
Nearpod	Online multimedia-presentation platform with multiple active-learning and collaborative opportunities. Student-performance data are kept in online reports
Padlet	Online digital tool to create walls to post text, videos, links and more for collaborative curating and brainstorming
Play Posit	Online tool to embed interactive questions in videos for active learning. The tool also allows uploading videos
Popplet	Online, collaborative graphic organizer or mind-mapping program for brainstorming rules, organizing concepts, cooperating and engaging in active learning
PowerPoint	Commonly used presentation and slides tool where interactive question slides can be added or used with other tools to increase interactivity
Quizizz	Interactive platform to create quizzes and live games for independent and collaborative learning activities and quiz games. The tool provides post-quiz reports
Quizlet/Quizlet Live	Interactive platform with flashcard-based interactive tools and games that students can use individually or in teams with Quizlet Live, a game-show-like competition
Response Cards	Low-tech strategy in which students hold up cards, signs or individual whiteboards to display their responses in synchronous lessons

Table 6.2 (Continued)

Technology	*Description*
Socrative and socrative PRO for higher education	Game-based online platform for questions, exit tickets, polls and more. It includes badges and scores for competitions, and it can create student-performance reports. The higher education version has additional features, e.g., the ability to support larger class sizes and more activities at once
Story Jumper	Online tool that lets students create multimedia books on course content.
Voice Thread	Interactive conversational platform and sharing tool for online multimedia presentations and student collaboration
Wakelet	Web-based platform for content curation (text, documents, videos, images, etc.). It can be used for individual or collaborative active learning across all content areas
Whiteboard.chat	Interactive, collaborative online whiteboard for brainstorming, sharing ideas, answering questions, and increasing active learning
Whiteboard.fi	Interactive, collaborative online whiteboard for brainstorming, sharing ideas, answering questions, and increasing active learning

Source: Barbetta (2023).

overcomes geographical barriers and promotes the inclusiveness of programs (Lall et al., 2023). Mentoring has been shown to improve the relationship between the mentor and mentee, as it enables a less structured dialog between them, which facilitates their relationship (Lall et al., 2023).

The importance of mentoring—especially its positive aspects in the relationship between the mentor and mentee, which are highlighted in the work at chapter 4—has led to the rise of numerous platforms for entrepreneurs to manage mentoring programs. Early studies evaluating the effectiveness of online mentoring for entrepreneurs highlighted the challenges of this practice, and they proposed frameworks to evaluate its effectiveness. Table 6.3 summarizes the beneficial aspects of online mentoring.

Table 6.3 Beneficial aspects of online mentoring

Positive aspect	*Perspective*	*Literature*
High levels of satisfaction with the program	Students	Broome et al. (2011); Jacobs et al. (2015)
Positive impacts on students' professional development	Students	Doyle et al. (2016); Jacobs et al. (2015)
Positive impacts on students' professional development	Faculty	Doyle et al. (2016)
Ability to use multiple means of communication	Students	Kumar and Coe (2017)
Peer groups (community) enhancing experience	Students	Broome et al. (2011); Jacobs et al. (2015); Kumar and Johnson (2017);
Positive impacts on faculty professional development	Faculty	Broome et al. (2011); Doyle et al. (2016);
Convenience and flexibility	Students	Andrew (2012);
Records of correspondence	Students	Andrew (2012
Scalability of mentoring	Faculty	de Beer and Mason (2009); Kumar and Johnson (2017);

6.2 The role of AI in entrepreneurship education

AI is emerging as one of the most disruptive contemporary innovations. This technology comes up as one of the most transformative forces in the education sector (Luan et al., 2020), and the integration of AI into educational processes is becoming an increasingly central topic in academia. Scholars are seeking to understand what education will look like on a global scale after the adoption of AI, especially in higher education (Limna et al., 2022).

In the education context, AI stands out for its ability to enhance learning through advanced personalization, monitoring, and assessment tools. AI applications in education, which are called "AIEd", range from intelligent tutoring systems and automated feedback mechanisms to predictive analytics for student-progress assessment, showed in Table 6.4. These systems represent a significant technological leap and introduce new methodological and pedagogical perspectives, thus reshaping the roles of teachers and learning processes (Chen et al., 2022).

To examine AI applications in the education sector, Holmes and Tuomi (2022) developed a taxonomy structured according to the target users (students or educators). Among the tools that are helpful for students, some can be identified that are also beneficial for entrepreneurship education; they are (1) intelligent tutoring systems, (2) dialog-based tutoring systems, (3) exploratory learning environments, (4) AI chatbots, and (5) AI-supported lifelong learning assistants.

Table 6.4 Benefits of AIEd technologies

AIEd technologies	*Benefits for learning and teaching*
Chatbot	• Stimulating conversations • Increased student interest
Expert systems	• Pedagogical planning • Use of learning management systems • Improved quality of interactions
Intelligent tutoring systems	• Personalized and timely materials, instructions and feedback • Customized learning experience based on needs, preferences and prior knowledge
Machine learning	• Large-scale student data analysis • Predictive models • Preventive and adaptive interventions
Personalized learning systems and environments	• Easier interactions • Improvement of e-learning • Customized materials and resources for tailored learning
Visualisation and virtual learning environments	• Collaborative learning, engagement and visual feedback • Information visualisation • Immersive learning environments

Source: Zhang and Aslan (2021).

6.2.1 Intelligent tutoring systems

These systems include applications that allow students to master complex skills (Wei, 2022) through the adaption of content as well as exercises and tests based on student interactions; these tools optimize the learning process based on highly personalized experiences. Some intelligent tutoring systems integrate learning-analytics tools and dashboards for teachers, thus allowing detailed monitoring of student learning processes. One example is the Assessment and Learning in Knowledge Spaces (ALEKS) platform. These systems are recognized as supportive of entrepreneurship because they enable the online practice of innovation and entrepreneurship to be strengthened (Wei, 2022).

6.2.2 Dialog-based tutoring systems

These systems simulate a dialog between the student and the tutor, with the goal of assisting the former in developing a deeper understanding of the topics being studied. Therefore, instead of passively absorbing information, students engage in an active-learning process that fosters critical thinking and problem-solving, which are key skills for entrepreneurs. One example is Watson education classroom by IBM. The advantages of dialog-based tutoring systems in entrepreneurship education are as follows:

i) **Active learning**: Instead of passively absorbing information, students engage in an active-learning process, which encourages critical thinking and problem-solving—key skills for an entrepreneur.
ii) **Building communication skills**: As they interact with the system, students enhance their communication and reasoning abilities, which are essential for entrepreneurs, who often need to pitch ideas, negotiate, and collaborate.
iii) **Immediate feedback**: Students receive instant feedback, allowing them to identify mistakes and improve in real time; this accelerates the learning process.

6.2.3 Exploratory learning environments

Compared to intelligent and dialog-based tutoring systems, exploratory learning environments (ELEs) offer students the opportunity to explore and manipulate the elements of the learning environment without a pre-established sequence. In terms of entrepreneurship education, ELEs foster creativity and innovation, which are crucial traits for entrepreneurial ventures where solutions often need to be discovered through trial and error. ELEs also provide hands-on experience. By experimenting with different scenarios and variables, students can get a sense of what practical application entails, which prepares them for real-world challenges. The advantages of ELEs in entrepreneurship education are as follows:

i) **Enhanced innovation**: This type of learning nurtures creativity and innovation, which are crucial traits for entrepreneurial ventures where solutions often need to be discovered through trial and error.
ii) **Hands-on experience**: By experimenting with different scenarios and variables, students get a sense of what practical application involves, which prepares them for the challenges of the real world.
iii) **Fostering problem-solving skills**: ELEs help students develop the ability to approach problems with flexible mindsets—an essential skill for entrepreneurs, who often encounter unpredictable business challenges.

The disadvantages of ELEs include the risk of cognitive overload and limited learning outcomes (Mavrikis et al., 2022).

6.2.4 AI chatbots

The use of AI-powered chatbots in education ranges from providing organizational support to students in areas such as academic services, facilities, exams, IT, and health care to employing chatbots as teaching assistants. Chatbots offer round-the-clock assistance, helping students get the information they need at any time, which is particularly useful for students balancing academic courses with entrepreneurial ventures. The advantages of AI chatbots in entrepreneurship education are as follows:

i) **Scalability**: These tools can handle large volumes of queries simultaneously, making them ideal for large classes and institutions.
ii) **Reduced human workload**: Chatbots can manage routine questions, allowing educators and assistants to focus on more complex and personalized tasks.

iii) **Increased student engagement**: Students feel more supported and engaged when they have immediate access to answers and resources.

6.2.5 AI-supported lifelong learning assistants

These tools, which are powered by large language models (LLMs; e.g., ChatGPT), are designed to engage with students 24/7 to enhance learning through personalized, on-demand support. They are easily integrated into mobile devices and offer flexible learning approaches, making them ideal for continuous education, especially for student entrepreneurs who need ongoing, personalized assistance. One example is ChatGPT. The benefits of AI-supported lifelong learning assistants in entrepreneurship education include the following:

i) **Continuous learning support**: Students receive ongoing assistance in their learning processes, which helps them stay motivated and on track; this is particularly beneficial for those with busy schedules.
ii) **Personalized feedback**: The system can adapt to the learning style and needs of each student, thereby ensuring that the help is relevant and useful.
iii) **24/7 availability**: These AI systems are always accessible, which is particularly helpful for entrepreneurs, who need flexible learning options that fit their hectic schedules.
iv) **Increased efficiency**: Students can access the help they need quickly, which makes the learning process more efficient and enables them to progress at their own pace.

6.3 The rise of generative AI and impacts on entrepreneurship education

Of particular relevance in the context of entrepreneurship education is generative AI, which is a subset of AI concerned with training models (LLMs) that can automatically generate content based on input data, such as text, graphics, audio and video (Lv 2023). LLMs imitate human learning processes by analyzing large data sets, acquiring knowledge from the patterns in these data and using this knowledge to generate new content with similarities to the original data (van Dis et al., 2023; Lim et al., 2023).

6.3.1 Learning opportunities with generative AI

Generative AI offers opportunities in education as it can enhance the learning experience and create personalized models of engagement (Atlas, 2023; Elbanna and Armstrong, 2024); it can also increase student engagement, interaction and collaborative learning (Kasneci et al., 2023).

Generative AI can have a role also in the context of students' entrepreneurial processes (Thanasi-Boçe and Hoxha, 2024). Early studies have shown that generative AI can become an integral part of an entrepreneur's capabilities, enabling them to develop and exploit opportunities as well as better disentangle themselves from the complexity of the ever-changing digital environment (Duong et al., 2025). Generative AI's accessibility and ability to maximize learning capabilities in the context of entrepreneurship enable the development of specific entrepreneurial skills, such as risk management, creativity, opportunity recognition, and critical thinking by means of enhanced prompting capabilities (Thanasi-Boçe & Hoxha, 2024).

Also relevant is the role of generative AI in the context of students' processes to create new ventures. AI can be a guide in entrepreneurship-related learning processes that enable improved venture-ideation skills. Generative AI offers opportunities in entrepreneurial education to enhance the learning experience and create personalized models of engagement (Atlas, 2023; Elbanna and Armstrong, 2024). Liu and Wang (2024) investigated undergraduate students who created start-ups using generative AI, and they found that this technology gave them tangible and intangible resources that facilitated collaboration and resulted in improved entrepreneurial performance.

6.3.2 The challenges of generative AI in education

Despite its many advantages, the integration of AI in entrepreneurship education also introduces potential challenges, which are ethical in nature and related to the impact on students' cognitive abilities.

Ethical concerns include the protection of privacy, potential bias in AI-generated content and the risk of over-reliance on technology. These concerns will require the development of new educational approaches based on the ability to critically evaluate the output of technology.

In this regard, the development of critical thinking and enquiry-based skills to appropriately interpret the information provided by AI is also necessary, with the aim of stimulating the critical awareness of students when they interact with AI tools (Bell and Bell, 2023). This aspect is directly related to the ability to ask effective questions to elicit relevant answers from AI models through prompting (Farrokhnia et al., 2024). This ability should become a skill that is taught in entrepreneurial education.

6.4 The rise of metaverse

Among the emerging technologies that are shaping the future of education, extended reality (XR) stands out for its ability to create highly interactive and immersive learning experiences, especially when combined with other new technologies, such as AI. XR encompasses VR, augmented reality (AR), and mixed reality; because, it blends digital and physical environments. This transforms the way students engage with content and allows them to interact with virtual spaces and objects based on more hands-on approaches to education, thus making complex concepts more tangible and enhancing student participation.

These technologies, along with blockchain, are also the basis for the creation of metaverse environments. The metaverse has attracted the attention of universities as a tool with transformative potential in entrepreneurship education. According to Park and Kim (2022), the term "metaverse" is a compound of "meta" (meaning "beyond") and "universe," and it refers to a three-dimensional virtual world in which avatars participate in political, economic, social, and cultural activities. In this sense, the metaverse is a shared virtual space that integrates physical and digital elements. The term "metaverse" has been used in various fields and has led to a new type of innovation by companies.

Recent studies have shown that in education, the metaverse can enhance learning capabilities and optimize online learning environments by simulating the physical experience in the digital world through the use of avatars as well as 3D and AR technologies. These technologies increase the emotional value of online experiences and, through XR systems (e.g., goggles), create connections to physical reality, thus strengthening student interaction and engagement (hype metaverse). Recently, scholars have also shown the interest of students, entrepreneurs and managers in the use of such technologies for education and work. For example, Espinoza-Guzmán et al. (2020)

found that 88.5% of students agreed that immersive technology was effective in their learning activities.

6.4.1 The metaverse in entrepreneurial learning

In the context of entrepreneurship, researchers have tested how the metaverse can act as a lever for the creation of new entrepreneurial ventures through the development of novel products and services (Calandra et al., 2023) and for the innovation of firms' business models (Kraus et al., 2022).

There is growing attention to the metaverse as a tool to enhance the effectiveness of entrepreneurship education. Early studies of the role of technology in students' learning processes provided empirical evidence that the metaverse can have a positive effect on such processes with regard to entrepreneurship (Espinoza-Guzmán et al., 2020). Abbadi's (2024) work has highlighted the central role of accessibility and simulation in metaverse technologies in learning processes. Simulations of real-world environments allow actual entrepreneurial challenges to be transferred to the digital realm and new ideas to be tested in risk-free settings; this creates experimentation hubs that foster innovation processes. Abbadi (2024) has also shown that participation in activities in the metaverse, such as avatar creation, virtual exploration, environmental design and social activism, promotes technological literacy and creativity, which provides people with the tools to innovate effectively in digital spaces. Calandra et al. (2023) have referred to the metaverse in education as "a living laboratory for digital applications."

6.4.2 Applications of the metaverse in entrepreneurial learning

The metaverse can also produce negative effects on learning processes. For example, a certain activity might be typical of the metaverse, and instead of promoting learning, it might distract attention (Abaddi, 2024). Some scholars have noted that the metaverse is still an underutilized technology. For instance, Maalaoui et al. (2025) analyzed a case of unsuccessful adoption of metaverse technology by academic institutions, highlighting the complexity of adoption processes and suggesting the creation of dedicated teams to manage them.

Another aspect to consider is the creation of appropriate models for the simulation of the physical experience through avatars. These models require investment in the infrastructure needed to access the metaverse (e.g., 360° cameras, virtual reality viewers, stabilizers, and motion detection systems), which will enable them to best mimic reality in the digital realm (Abaddi, 2024).

Furthermore, the use of technologies in the metaverse, such as XR and AR, requires universities to have teachers with the technical knowledge to use these tools as methods. Universities must provide faculty with the necessary skills and develop appropriate methodologies to manage e-learning processes in the metaverse.

6.5 Towards the eduverse in entrepreneurial learning

Regarding the technological changes driven by XR, it is appropriate to dwell on the concept of the "eduverse", which has gradually taken shape with the advancement of digital tools and the growing demand for more interactive, flexible, and personalized education. The term "eduverse" is a portmanteau of "education" and "universe," and it defines an ecosystem that combines cutting-edge technologies, including AI, VR and data analytics (Okewu et al., 2021). Its most recent version is the eduverse 2.0 (Damaševičius and Zailskaite-Jakste, 2024), which leverages systems powered by AI to offer personalized learning paths and adaptive tutoring (Damaševičius & Sidekerskiene, 2024). While AI plays the previously explained role in the analysis of students' progress, the delivery of personalized content and the optimization of instructional strategies in real time (Wang et al., 2023), XR applications bring subjects to life by enabling students to visualize and interact with digital models, thereby fostering a deeper understanding of abstract topics.

In education, XR supports various learning methods, including observational, operational and social learning, as well as academic research. It has applications in smart education product design, game-based learning, the creation of intelligent learning environments, and special education (Pregowska et al., 2024). Furthermore, XR technology has proven effective in a wide range of subjects, such as biology, arts, language, music, health care, and physical education, making it a versatile tool for diverse educational contexts (Jagatheesaperumal et al., 2024).

One of the significant advantages of XR is its portability and scalability, as it provides a flexible, easily accessible solution that can be distributed widely; it also allows for standardized, repeatable learning experiences without the need for in-person instructors

(Memmesheimer & Ebert, 2022). The immersive nature of XR also enhances spatial awareness and learning contextualization, making it easier for students to connect theoretical knowledge with practical, real-world issues (Logeswaran et al., 2021).

As XR technology continues to evolve, its potential to reshape educational environments will become even more pronounced, making education more dynamic and accessible to students across the globe.

6.6 Conclusions

The integration of new technologies, such as AI, into education marks the shift from traditional learning models, which focus on theoretical knowledge or "learning about," to experiential and immersive learning approaches. These approaches emphasize the acquisition of multidisciplinary knowledge that fosters the development of creativity, analytical thinking, and critical thinking (Gafni et al., 2024). Enabling technologies can enhance entrepreneurial practice by creating protected environments where students can develop and test their ideas, thus stimulating the transition from aptitude to the formation of new ventures. In addition, digital technologies can overcome the physical limits of learning by promoting experimentation in remote locations and stimulating students' connection with the business community, which generates inclusivity in entrepreneurship education. However, the integration of enabling technologies into entrepreneurial learning also faces many challenges. These are related to the skills and resources that universities need to incorporate these technologies into their curricula, and to manage the potential negative impacts on learning processes.

References

Abaddi, S. (2024). "Metaverse, entrepreneurial learning and opportunity exploitation", *Journal of Entrepreneurship in Emerging Economies*. Vol. 17 No. 3, pp. 744–773

Akintayo, O.T., Eden, C.A., Ayeni, O.O. and Onyebuchi, N.C. (2024). "Integrating AI with emotional and social learning in primary education: Developing a holistic adaptive learning ecosystem", *Computer Science & IT Research Journal*, *5*(5), pp. 1076–1089.

Atlas, S. (2023). "ChatGPT for higher education and professional development: A guide to conversational AI." *College of Business Faculty Publications*. https://digitalcommons.uri.edu/cba_facpubs/548.

Barbetta, P.M. (2023). "Technologies as tools to increase active learning during online higher-education instruction", *Journal of Educational Technology Systems*, Vol. 51, No. 3, pp. 317–339.

Bell, R. and Bell, H. (2023). "Entrepreneurship education in the era of generative artificial intelligence", *Entrepreneurship Education*, Vol. 6, No. 3, pp. 229–244.

Bradley, V.M. (2021). "Learning management system (LMS) use with online instruction", *International Journal of Technology in Education*, Vol. 4, No. 1, pp. 68–92.

Broome, M. E., Halstead, J. A., Pesut, D. J., Rawl, S. M., & Boland, D. L. (2011). Evaluating the outcomes of a distance-accessible PhD program. *Journal of professional nursing : official journal of the American Association of Colleges of Nursing*, *27*(2), 69–77. https://doi.org/10.1016/j.profnurs.2010.09.011

Calandra, D., Oppioli, M., Sadraei, R., Jafari-Sadeghi, V. and Biancone, P.P. (2023). "Metaverse meets digital entrepreneurship: A practitioner-based qualitative synthesis", *International Journal of Entrepreneurial Behavior & Research*, Vol. 30, No. 2/3, pp. 666–686.

Chen, X., Zou, D. and Xie, H. (2020). "Fifty years of British Journal of Educational Technology: A topic modeling based bibliometric perspective", *British Journal of Educational Technology*, Vol. 51, No. 3, pp. 692–708.

Chen, X., Zou, D., Xie, H., Cheng, G. and Liu, C. (2022). "Two decades of artificial intelligence in education", *Educational Technology & Society*, Vol. 25, No. 1, pp. 28–47.

Criollo-C, S., Govea, J., Játiva, W., Pierrottet, J., Guerrero-Arias, A., Jaramillo-Alcázar, Á. and Luján-Mora, S. (2023). "Towards the integration of emerging technologies as support for the teaching and learning model in higher education", *Sustainability*, Vol. 15, No. 7, 6055.

Damaševičius, R. and Sidekerskienė, T. (2024). "Virtual worlds for learning in metaverse: A narrative review", *Sustainability*, Vol. 16, No. 5, 2032.

Damaševišius, R. and Zailskaitė-Jakštė, L. (2024). "Question, explore, discover (QED): A new paradigm for learning in the AI era". In *General Aspects of Applying Generative AI in Higher Education: Opportunities and Challenges* (pp. 221–240). Springer Nature Switzerland.

de Beer, M., & Mason, R. (2009). Using a blended approach to facilitate postgraduate supervision. *Innovations in Education and Teaching International*, Vol. 46, No. 2, 213–226

Doyle, N., Jacobs, K., & Ryan, C. (2016). Faculty Mentors' Perspectives on E-Mentoring Post-Professional Occupational Therapy Doctoral Students. *Occupational therapy international*, Vol. *23, No.* 4, pp. 305–317. https://doi.org/10.1002/oti.1431

Duong, C.D., Nguyen, T.H., Ngo, T.V.N., Pham, T.T.P., Vu, A.T. and Dang, N.S. (2025). "Using generative artificial intelligence (ChatGPT) for travel purposes: Parasocial interaction and tourists' continuance intention", *Tourism Review*, Vol. 80, No. 4, pp. 813–827.

Eastern Peak (2025). "10 edtech startups ideas for education entrepreneurs in 2025" report available at https://easternpeak.com/blog/edtech-startup-ideas-for-education-entrepreneurs/.

Elbanna, S. and Armstrong, L. (2024). "Exploring the integration of ChatGPT in education: Adapting for the future", *Management & Sustainability: An Arab Review*, Vol. 3, No. 1, pp. 16–29.

Espinoza-Guzmán, L.V., García-Herrera, D.G., Erazo-Álvarez, J.C. and Narváe–Zurita, C.I. (2020). "Immersive education for entrepreneurship and management disciplines: Metaverse's experience", *Metaverse*, Vol. 1, No. 1, p. 8.

Farrokhnia, M., Banihashem, S.K., Noroozi, O. and Wals, A. (2024). "A SWOT analysis of ChatGPT: Implications for educational practice and research", *Innovations in Education and Teaching International*, Vol. 61, No. 3, pp. 460–474.

Fernández, A., Gómez, B., Binjaku, K., and Meçe, E.K. (2023). "Digital transformation initiatives in higher education institutions: A multivocal literature review", *Education and Information Technologies*, Vol. 28, No. 10, pp. 12351–12382.

Gafni, R., Aviv, I., Kantsepolsky, B., Sherman, S., Rika, H., Itzkovich, Y., and Barger, A. (2024). "Objectivity by design: The impact of AI-driven approach on employees' soft skills evaluation", *Information and Software Technology*, Vol. 170, 107430.

Hamilton, M. (2021). "Envisioning education 4.0—a scenario planning approach to predicting the future". In *Future directions in digital information* (pp. 267–283). Chandos Publishing.

Hobson, Andrew. (2012). Fostering Face-to-face Mentoring and Coaching. 10.4135/9781446247549.n5. In The SAGE Handbook of Mentoring and Coaching in Education, pp.59-73. SAGE Publishing.

Holmes, W. and Tuomi, I. (2022). "State of the art and practice in AI in education", *European Journal of Education*, Vol. 57, No. 4, pp. 542–570.

ISTE. (2017) International Society for Technology in Education Standards for Educators. https://cdn.iste.org/www-root/Downloads/Downloads/Download-4070.pdf

Jacobs, Karen & Doyle, Nancy & Ryan, Cathryn. (2015). The Nature, Perception, and Impact of e-Mentoring on Post-Professional Occupational Therapy Doctoral Students. *Occupational therapy in health care*. Vol. 29. 10.3109/07380577.2015.1006752.

Jagatheesaperumal, S.K., Ahmad, K., Al-Fuqaha, A. and Qadir, J. (2024). "Advancing education through extended reality and internet of everything enabled metaverses: Applications, challenges, and open issues", *IEEE Transactions on Learning Technologies*, Vol. 17, pp. 1120–1139.

Johansson-Sköldberg, U., Woodilla, J. and Çetinkaya, M. (2013). "Design thinking: Past, present and possible futures", *Creativity and Innovation Management*, Vol. 22, No. 2, pp. 121–146.

Kasneci, E., Seßler, K., Küchemann, S., Bannert, M., Dementieva, D., Fischer, F. ... and Kasneci, G. (2023). "ChatGPT for good? On opportunities and challenges of large language models for education", *Learning and Individual Differences*, Vol. 103, 102274.

Kraus, S., Kanbach, D.K., Krysta, P.M., Steinhoff, M.M. and Tomini, N. (2022). "Facebook and the creation of the metaverse: Radical business model innovation or incremental transformation?", *International Journal of Entrepreneurial Behavior & Research*, Vol. 28, No. 9, pp. 52–77.

Kumar, S., & Coe, C. (2017). Mentoring and Student Support in Online Doctoral Programs. *American Journal of Distance Education,* Vol. 31, No. 2, pp. 128–142. https://doi.org/10.1080/08923647.2017.1300464

Kumar, S., & Johnson, M. (2017). Mentoring Doctoral Students Online: Mentor Strategies and Challenges. *Mentoring & Tutoring: Partnership in Learning,* Vol. 25, pp. 202-222. https://doi.org/10.1080/13611267.2017.1326693

Lackéus, M. (2015). "*Entrepreneurship in education: What, why, when, how* (No. 2015/6)". OECD Publishing.

Lall, S.A., Chen, L.W., and Mason, D.P. (2023). "Digital platforms and entrepreneurial support: A field experiment in online mentoring", *Small Business Economics*, Vol. 61, No. 2, pp. 631–654.

Lim, S. and Schmälzle, R. (2023). "Artificial intelligence for health message generation: An empirical study using a large language model (LLM) and prompt engineering", *Frontiers in Communication*, Vol. 8, 1129082.

Limna, P., Jakwatanatham, S., Siripipattanakul, S., Kaewpuang, P. and Sriboonruang, P. (2022). "A review of artificial intelligence (AI) in education during the digital era", *Advance Knowledge for Executives*, Vol. 1, No. 1, pp. 1–9.

Liu, A. and Wang, S. (2024). "Generative artificial intelligence (GenAI) and entrepreneurial performance: Implications for entrepreneurs", *The Journal of Technology Transfer*, Vol. 49, No. 6, pp. 2389–2412.

Logeswaran, A., Munsch, C., Chong, Y.J., Ralph, N. and McCrossnan, J. (2021). "The role of extended reality technology in healthcare education: Towards a learner-centred approach", *Future Healthcare Journal*, Vol. 8, No. 1, pp. e79–e84.

Luan, H., Geczy, P., Lai, H., Gobert, J., Yang, S.J., Ogata, H., ... and Tsai, C.C. (2020). "Challenges and future directions of big data and artificial intelligence in education", *Frontiers in Psychology*, Vol. 11, 580820.

Lv, Z. (2023). "Generative artificial intelligence in the metaverse era," *Cognitive Robotics*, vol. 3, no. May, pp. 208–217.

Maalaoui, A., Mejri, I.B.G., Loarne, L.S.L. and Kallmuenzer A. (2025) "Entrepreneurial education in the metaverse: Challenges and prospects for business schools", *International Journal of Entrepreneurship and Innovation*. Vol. 26. No 1, pp. 85–95. https://doi.org/10.1177/14657503251314365

Masalimova, A.R., Khvatova, M.A., Chikileva, L.S., Zvyagintseva, E.P., Stepanova, V.V. and Melnik, M.V. (2022). "Distance learning in higher education during COVID-19", *Frontiers in Education*, Vol. 7, 822958.

Mavrikis, M., Rummel, N., Wiedmann, M., Loibl, K. and Holmes, W. (2022). "Combining exploratory learning with structured practice educational technologies to foster both conceptual and procedural fractions knowledge", *Educational Technology Research and Development*, Vol. 70, No. 3, pp. 691–712.

Memmesheimer, V. M. and Ebert, A. (2022). "Scalable extended reality: A future research agenda", *Big Data and Cognitive Computing*, Vol. 6, No. 1, p. 12.

Okewu, E., Adewole, P., Misra, S., Maskeliunas, R. and Damasevicius, R. (2021). "Artificial neural networks for educational data mining in higher education: A systematic literature review", *Applied Artificial Intelligence*, Vol. 35, No. 13, pp. 983–1021.

Osterwalder, A. and Pigneur, Y. (2010). "*Business model generation: A handbook for visionaries, game changers, and challengers*". Wiley.

Park, S. and Kim, S. (2022). "Identifying world types to deliver gameful experiences for sustainable learning in the metaverse", *Sustainability*, Vol. 14, No. 3, p. 1361.

Pregowska, A., Osial, M. and Gajda, A. (2024). "What will the education of the future look like? How have metaverse and extended reality affected the higher education systems?", *Metaverse Basic and Applied Research*, Vol. 3, p. 1.

Rahmatullah, A.S., Mulyasa, E., Syahrani, S., Pongpalilu, F. and Putri, R.E. (2022). "Digital era 4.0: The contribution to education and student psychology", *Linguistics and Culture Review*, Vol. 6, No. 3, pp. 89–107.

Sarasvathy, S.D. (2001). "Causation and effectuation: Toward a theoretical shift from economic inevitability to entrepreneurial contingency", *Academy of management Review*, Vol, 26, No. 2, pp. 243–263.

Sarasvathy, S.D. and Dew, N. (2005). "New market creation through transformation", *Journal of Evolutionary Economics*, Vol. 15, pp. 533–565.

Sarasvathy, S.D. and Venkataraman, S. (2011). "Entrepreneurship as method: Open questions for an entrepreneurial future", *Entrepreneurship Theory and Practice*, Vol. 35, No. 1, pp. 113–135.

Thanasi-Boçe, M. and Hoxha, J. (2024). "Blockchain and AI-driven framework for measuring the digital economy in GCC", *Emerging Science Journal*, Vol. 8, No. 4, pp. 1554–1582.

Van Dis, E.A., Bollen, J., Zuidema, W., Van Rooij, R. and Bockting, C.L. (2023). "ChatGPT: Five priorities for research", *Nature*, Vol. 614, No. 7947, pp. 224–226.

Wang, S., Sun, Z. and Chen, Y. (2023). "Effects of higher education institutes' artificial intelligence capability on students' self-efficacy, creativity and learning performance", *Education and Information Technologies*, Vol. 28, No. 5, pp. 4919–4939.

Wardoyo, C., Narmaditya, B.S., Qurrata, V.A., Satrio, Y.D. and Sahid, S. (2025). "Are students ready for digital business? Antecedents of entrepreneurial intentions among Indonesian students using a serial mediation," *Social Sciences & Humanities Open*, Vol. 11, 101213.

Wei, M. (2022). "The design of intelligent tutoring systems using college students' innovation and entrepreneurship education under the background of online teaching," *Wireless Communications and Mobile Computing*, Vol. 2022, No. 1, 9180933.

Zhang, K. and Aslan, A.B. (2021). "AI technologies for education: Recent research & future directions", *Computers and Education: Artificial intelligence*, Vol. 2, 100025.

Conclusion

This book explored the phenomenon of student entrepreneurship in Europe, highlighting the main factors that drive the transformation of a student into an entrepreneur, as well as the relevant barriers, with a focus on the role of entrepreneurship education. What emerges from the volume is the key role of entrepreneurship education in Europe. Despite having established itself later in Europe than in America, this type of education has led to the creation of courses specifically dedicated to the development of entrepreneurship and the promotion of initiatives aimed at increasing students' capacity to found new businesses, especially in geographic contexts close to innovation ecosystems.

In this process, universities have managed to establish themselves as key regional catalysts for the creation of new entrepreneurial ventures, thus significantly influencing students' attitudes and intentions towards entrepreneurship.

By analyzing and systematizing experiences of entrepreneurship education in higher education, the book showed how universities have become active players in knowledge transfer processes and have activated practical experiences based on the new experiential approaches to entrepreneurship that use "learning by doing," thus fostering connections between the business world and education. In this way, universities become central nodes in European innovation ecosystems.

In addition, the benchmarking analysis of entrepreneurship courses across Europe allowed for the construction of a model of entrepreneurship education at the European level, which is grounded on the following factors:

DOI: 10.4324/9781003607649-8

1. The integration of theoretical knowledge with practical and experiential activities, which nurtures the development of enquiry-based skills.
2. The inclusion of soft skills development, with particular attention to creativity, critical thinking, communication, and negotiation abilities.
3. A high level of international student mobility, which is achieved through participation in projects with foreign companies or studying at partner universities abroad.
4. External exposure through participation in business challenges, testimonials, and solution-creation activities.
5. Learning-by-doing activities, including involvement in internships at start-ups, established companies and consulting firms, which foster entrepreneurial skills.

Furthermore, by exploring the European project ENTREPRENEDU, the volume presented new practices for accelerating student entrepreneurship. It identified the key aspects of a venture-building syllabus that can be replicated in other educational settings and linked to mentoring activities and other innovative practices (e.g., hackathons) to promote venture building.

The practical cases revealed how experiential tools have a leading role in promoting ventures by students. Also relevant is the creation of collaborative learning environments that equip students with practical skills and proactive mindsets. The ENTREPRENEDU project shows that these tools are effective in promoting venture building, especially in regions with a low rate of entrepreneurship, as they create the necessary conditions to transfer skills and confidence to start businesses, thus generating local employment and diversifying economic activities.

The development of digitalization has increased the opportunities for practical experimentation and introduced new pedagogical tools that enhance learning processes. In particular, emerging technologies such as blockchain, the metaverse and AI can provide the institutions responsible for entrepreneurial education with activities and tools for the simulation of scenarios as well as the generation and experimentation of new entrepreneurial ideas, thus accelerating learning processes and interactions between teachers and students. This can create the conditions to strengthen students' abilities to create new ventures.

However, the effects of these new technologies on the development of entrepreneurial skills remain under-explored in the literature, and their adoption in European universities is still limited. Increased adoption would require universities to equip themselves with adequate infrastructure and skills to manage the integration of these technologies into learning environments.

The volume also highlights the importance of incorporating experiential and practical activities into courses and international exposure, which requires the creation of partnerships with actors in the ecosystem of start-ups and training institutions at the international level. In this regard, the European Universities alliances promoted by the EU could represent a useful support for creating networks capable of leveraging technology to enhance the processes of venture creation by young innovators.

Index

Made in the USA
Las Vegas, NV
19 September 2026

d9634ab7-cbac-4588-aa7d-c0967d0ac46fR01